The Catholic Guide to Miracles

Adam Blai

The Catholic Guide to Miracles

Separating the Authentic from the Counterfeit

SOPHIA INSTITUTE PRESS
Manchester, New Hampshire

Cover design by David Ferris (www.davidferrisdesign.com).

On the cover: *Walking on Water*, by Ivan Aivazovsky, public domain, image courtesy of Wikimedia Commons.

Sophia Institute Press
Box 5284, Manchester, NH 03108
1-800-888-9344

www.SophiaInstitute.com

Library of Congress Cataloging-in-Publication Data

Names: Blai, Adam C., 1970- author.
Title: The Catholic guide to miracles : separating the authentic from the counterfeit / Adam Blai.
Description: Manchester, New Hampshire : Sophia Institute Press, [2021] | Includes bibliographical references. | Summary: "Explores various miracles, from biblical times to modern times, including miraculous healings, apparitions, the Stigmata, levitation, incorruptiblity, and Eucharistic miracles, and also looks at human and demonic counterfeits"— Provided by publisher.
Identifiers: LCCN 2021003844 | ISBN 9781644132968 (paperback) | ISBN 9781644132975 (ebook)
Subjects: LCSH: Miracles. | Catholic Church—Doctrines.
Classification: LCC BT97.3 .B53 2021 | DDC 231.7/3—dc23
LC record available at https://lccn.loc.gov/2021003844

First printing

For my mother, and all mothers,
for saying yes to the first miracle
we all experience: life

Contents

Introduction

Our fascination with miracles is inextricably tied up with our fear of death. Miracles give us hope for preservation from suffering and, ultimately, an escape from death. They not only give us hope for a short-term solution to a problem facing us, but more importantly, they reveal the reality of God and so give us hope for the ultimate solution to the problem of death.

When we face our death, either in our imagination or in reality, our minds struggle. The mind cannot imagine not being, and this creates anxiety, very often the central fear in our lives. While most creatures can focus on only the here and now—the fundamental tasks of eating, fighting, and reproducing, which keep their species alive—humans can reflect on the past and imagine the future. This ability allows us to pass on knowledge to the next generation, save for retirement, and apply science to the questions of the universe. It also means that we spend some time in the present lamenting the past and worrying about the future. It means we contemplate, and sometimes obsess over, our death.

Mortality is a threat that we cannot fight or run away from. We know that, at least in earthly terms, we are and will be defeated by it. In the absence of religious belief, we find various solutions: denial, distraction, existential crisis, despair, and so on.

The central promise of Christianity is that Jesus Christ defeated death and provides a solution to this apparently impossible problem. The proof of this promise is that Jesus vanquished death on the Cross and rose on the third day. As St. Paul says,

> And if Christ has not been raised, then empty [too] is our preaching; empty, too, your faith. (1 Cor. 15:14)

The Gospels describe a number of miracles that Jesus performed as proofs of His divinity: healings, exorcisms, resurrections, control over nature, and forgiveness of sins. All of these proved Christ's divine identity in the Jewish worldview—that He had powers, including over suffering, sin, and death, that no purely human person could have. These miracles, therefore, are among the central proofs of Christianity.

It is important, though, to define *miracle* carefully. To do this, we need a quick background in epistemology—the study of how we come to know things. St. Thomas Aquinas points out in the *Summa Contra Gentiles*[1] that a miracle is essentially something we cannot explain. That's easy enough. When we cannot explain something, we wonder about it, maybe even experience a sense of awe. There are some events that are awe-inspiring to some but mundane to others: seeing a faraway planet might be incredible for a child but commonplace for an astronomer. Thomas addresses this by saying that a true miracle is something that has a cause that is absolutely hidden from everyone, and that nobody, no matter how knowledgeable, can explain.

Thomas then organizes miracles into three ranks. Miracles of the first rank are things done by God that nature can never do,

[1] St. Thomas Aquinas, *Summa Contra Gentiles* (Notre Dame: University of Notre Dame Press, 1975), bk. 3, par. 101.

such as the raising of Lazarus, who had been dead in the tomb for four days. Miracles of the second rank are things done by God that are natural, but not in the way He accomplishes them. It is natural for a person to see, but not for a person to see after having been born blind. Miracles of the third rank are things done by God that nature can do, but without the usual natural limitations. In time, a high fever usually passes, but sometimes God cures a fever instantly. For Thomas, anything done by the power of any creature cannot be a miracle; only acts done by God can be. This means that anything done by an angel, or a fallen angel, cannot be a miracle, as they are creatures.

In the Old Testament, God primarily performed miracles to reward or to punish people—but His miracles also advanced His will for the world and the people in it. In the New Testament, we mostly see Jesus performing miracles that were proofs beyond His words of who He was. These miracles involved His healing and freeing people from their physical and spiritual shackles. The central miracle of His life, of course, was His Resurrection, by which He conquered death and freed people from it.

We continue to see miracles in our time. We hear stories of amazing healings, apparitions of Mary, Eucharistic miracles, heavenly near-death experiences, angels appearing, and other wonderful events. In our scientific age, though, it has also become easier to dismiss these accounts, appealing to fields such as neuroscience to explain away the seemingly unexplainable. It has also become easier to fabricate audio and video evidence with computers, making good objective proof of miracles even more important—and harder to come by. This is why medical miracles, which can be substantiated by reliable objective medical data, are those most relied on for the causes of saints.

The unsolvable problem remains, though: we have not solved death. We can avoid it and distract ourselves with shallow stimulation, substances, and the ego, but eventually death intrudes. Someone dear to us passes, we get older, or we get distressingly sick. This helps explain the common pattern of drifting away from religion as a seemingly invincible young adult but returning later in life. Our egos cannot defeat death alone, and so, on some level, we find that we need God between us and death.

My professional background is in therapy and evaluation in forensic settings and my research background is in brain science, specifically brain-wave analysis. Building on this experience for about fifteen years, I have been increasingly involved as a lay consultant in exorcisms (called a peritus, or "expert," in religious demonology and exorcism for the Pittsburgh Diocese). I have both attended and helped at hundreds of solemn exorcisms and taught at national conferences on exorcism for more than a decade. Although only priests can perform the rite of exorcism with permission from their bishop, I participate by screening potential demoniacs for mental health conditions, ensuring that the victim of demonic attack is prepared for and stable during the exorcism, and coaching the exorcists when needed: I might explain what a demon is doing and what the best response is. Finally, I get calls from exorcist friends and dioceses all over the country about the exorcism ministry and specific cases.

My confidence in the supernatural is not only based on faith but has been built through years of extraordinary experiences and observations. Medical doctors and mental health professionals who work with those in our care also sometimes have their worldview shaken by the spiritual realities they see and so cannot deny. I want to be a rational person, and the truth is that, given what I have seen, it would be *irrational* to deny the spiritual world. I have come to a place where I have to say that for me it is all real. God is real. Angels and demons are real. The spiritual world is real. Jesus Christ is alive and present as I write this, and with you as you read it. I have seen too much evidence to deny it. But, I know that most people have not seen. I know that most people have some faith, but they hunger for their own proofs.

This book on miracles is not meant to be merely a collection of pious stories, but one of analysis and personal sharing. How were things validated in the past? How are they validated now? What are the proofs, and why should we believe them? Some of the events recounted here are so old that we have to choose whether to trust those who were there and wrote down their experiences. One of the many positive aspects of science and modern medicine is that they have sometimes provided objective scientific proofs that were not available before. We now have more than pious testimony in some cases. So, let us look at the miracles of the past and the ones in our modern age and see if we can find signs that we can hold on to and that point to God.

1

The History of Miracles and Their Definitions

The Old Testament

The first act of God recorded in Scripture is a miracle: the creation of the universe. The rules of nature were established at that moment. Physics continues to seek an understanding of the first moment of creation, and interestingly seems to be positing, as the Scriptures relate, that the universe likely sprang out of nothing.

In the first creation account in the first chapter of Genesis, God created human beings on the sixth day. In the second account, in the second chapter, we meet the first humans: Adam and Eve. Everything and everyone was perfectly obedient to God—until our first parents disobeyed Him. After the Fall, Adam and Eve were cast out of the Garden of Eden and reduced: their relationship with nature and their own bodies became adversarial. They would toil for food, grow old and sick, feel pain, and die. Most importantly, their direct personal relationship with God was broken. God had walked with them in the garden personally, but they lost that direct access. The restoration of that direct access is the entire purpose of Jesus' coming into the world and healing that rift.

We then read the very long history of people living in this world largely cut off from God: in nearly constant conflict with each other. During this history God sometimes talked with prophets, in visions or dreams, in order to guide people through critical times. God also performed miracles in response to the pleas of holy people, such as Elijah and Elisha. Sometimes God performed public and dramatic miracles for the prophets to convince the people to pay attention to them. These included healing the sick, raising the dead, and the dramatic fire from heaven that consumed the sacrifice Elijah presented to God in his challenge to the priests of Baal (1 Kings 18:36–40).

When God wanted to bring His Chosen People to the Promised Land, He spent many years in a more direct interaction with them, largely through the mediation of Moses. God appeared to Moses personally and talked with him directly. He used Moses to tell the Egyptians to release the Jews from slavery so they could return to Israel. When the Egyptians refused, God sent the ten plagues, which were dramatic and punishing miracles that eventually convinced them to let the Israelites go. When the Jews were wandering in the desert, God fed them with manna from Heaven, which appeared every morning on the ground. When the Jews violated the First Commandment and worshipped false gods, the true God punished them with miraculous negative events.

> I am the LORD your God, who brought you out of the land of Egypt, out of the house of bondage. You shall have no other gods before me. You shall not make for yourself a graven image, or any likeness of anything that is in heaven above, or that is in the earth beneath, or that is in the water under the earth; you shall not bow down to them or serve them. (Ex 20:2–5; cf. Deut 5:6–9)

> It is written: "You shall worship the Lord your God and him only shall you serve" (Mt 4:10).[2]

The New Testament

When God wished to come into the world and speak face-to-face with humanity again, He came as the Word Incarnate, Jesus Christ, the second Person of the Blessed Trinity. In the accounts of Christ's life, there is a great emphasis on His miracles, which were important both in themselves and in the reactions they provoked in those around Him.

Many people heard of Jesus curing the sick and the possessed, and they wanted to see these miracles for themselves; they wanted to be healed. Jesus knew the importance of miracles as signs of the presence of God, as we read in John 4:48:

> Jesus said to him, "Unless you people see signs and wonders, you will not believe."

The story of Jesus culminates with His death on the Cross and His Resurrection from the dead three days later. This is the central miracle of Christianity, the sacrifice that reopened the way to God, which had been closed off by the Fall of Adam and Eve. That is why the primary symbol of Catholic Christianity is the crucifix: Christ on the Cross at the moment of the redemptive sacrifice that saved the world.

After Christ died and rose, there was a great miracle at Pentecost, when Jesus sent the apostles the Holy Spirit. The apostles

[2] *Catechism of the Catholic Church* (CCC), article 1, the First Commandment, https://www.vatican.va/archive/ccc_css/archive/catechism/p3s2c1a1.htm.

immediately preached to the people and were understood by everyone in the crowd, even though they spoke many languages. After this, the apostles started performing many miracles and signs of their own. These miracles included Peter's healing a lame man (Acts 3:1–8), healing palsy (Acts 9:33–34), and raising the dead (Acts 9:36–41); Paul's healing a cripple (Acts 14:8–10), casting out a spirit of divination (Acts 16:16–18), and raising the dead (Acts 20:9–12); and many others. Their preaching and their miracles established the Church in the world.

Heavenly Intercessors

From the very beginning of the Church, Christians have looked for and recognized miracles in their midst. These extraordinary phenomena were never expected to be restricted to biblical times: the Church has always understood that God remains active in our lives until the end of time and beyond. Furthermore, from the earliest days of the Church, it was understood that prayer to heavenly intercessors — the saints and angels — was efficacious. And so, when a person died a martyr for the Faith or lived a notably holy life, he or she might be venerated by a local group and, eventually, by the universal Church. It is important to understand that this is not worshipping saints or angels but asking them to pray for our intentions, since they have a direct access to God that we do not have.

The process of canonization has developed substantially over the years. The Church has desired to formalize the process and take advantage of modern science. In the early Church, a popular holy man or woman would simply be acclaimed a saint by the faithful, and devotions and feasts would develop organically. Today, in order to give the faithful confidence in the heavenly status of a saint, the Church goes through a process of canonization. When the Church declares someone a saint, it means that we can be sure that person is in heaven and can intercede for us with the Lord. So we can venerate that person, build churches in his or her honor, memorialize the person in the Mass, and include him or her in the calendar of the Church.

The canonization process begins with an investigation by the local bishop of the proposed saint, usually starting no sooner than five years after the person has died. This investigation includes everything the person wrote or recorded, the testimony of those who knew him or her, and much more. If the investigation finds that the person lived a heroic life of virtue, the cause is turned over to the Congregation for the Causes of Saints in Rome. The Congregation then gives the person the title Servant of God, which indicates that the person is being investigated; it does not mean there can be any public veneration of the person.

The Congregation then appoints a postulator to oversee the cause, and further research is done with a focus on the virtues of faith, hope, charity, prudence, justice, fortitude, and temperance. If the investigation continues to be favorable, the Congregation may ask the pope to grant the person the title Venerable, at which point the person's body is exhumed for examination and for relics to be collected. A relic can be part of the person's body, or his or her possession, such as clothing. The faithful are encouraged to ask the potential saint to intercede for them in serious matters in the pious hope that a miracle will occur in connection with the intercession of the potential saint.

If there is a documented miracle, almost always a healing, the Congregation may ask the pope to declare the person Blessed. Alternatively, this declaration can occur without a miracle if the person died a martyr. Beatification means that although veneration has not yet been approved for the universal Church, it is considered worthy of belief that the person is in Heaven. The Church designates a feast day on the calendar of the blessed's home diocese or religious order but not for the universal Church.

These confirmatory miracles are almost always healings because healings are the easiest to substantiate. The Church's standards for a miraculous healing are as follows:

1. It must be spontaneous: the healing must have occurred on its own, and not in response to some external action such as a medical treatment. Healings often occur after all medical interventions have stopped, so there is no way to explain them.
2. It must be instantaneous: the healing must have happened all at one moment, or very quickly. Miraculous healings do not look like normal biological processes, such as gradually getting over an illness.
3. It must be complete: the healing cannot be partial. A miraculous healing of hearing, for instance, would involve the full range of normal healing for the person's age, not only hearing faintly.
4. It must be enduring: the healing cannot be a brief respite from illness, but must be a permanent healing that endures for years.
5. Doctors can provide no natural explanation; medical science does not know a mechanism that could have caused the healing.

Finally, usually after many years of study, prayer, and investigation, and if the Congregation can confirm a second miracle (or a single miracle for a martyr), the man or woman may be canonized—declared a saint of the universal Church. This means the faithful can be certain in their devotions that they are praying to a member of the Church Triumphant in Heaven. A feast day for the saint is created in the calendar of the universal Church, and churches can be named for him or her.

Miraculous healings are the central proofs for being declared a saint precisely because they can be performed only by God. Therefore, if a miracle happens in response to prayer to an intercessor, we know that that intercessor is with God in Heaven. Let us consider some of the many miraculous healings used to declare people saints.

2

Miraculous Healings

The most rigorously investigated miraculous healings are those that are submitted as evidence for beatification and canonization. As we have seen, for a healing to be considered miraculous, it must be spontaneous, instantaneous, complete, lasting, and unexplainable by modern medicine. All of the material related to the purported miracle is first studied by the postulator of the cause for sainthood. This involves gathering all the medical data and consulting competent medical experts in the relevant specialties. Then the dossier is submitted to the Holy See, which scrutinizes it closely and potentially investigates further. There must be no room for doubt about a potential miracle used to beatify or canonize a person. Therefore, the miracles that have been accepted for beatifications and canonizations are the best examples of miraculous healings we have. We will focus on these miracles.

Sts. Francisco and Jacinta Marto

Francisco and Jacinta Marto were two of the three visionaries of Fatima in 1916 and 1917. The story of Fatima and the miracle of the sun is common knowledge and so will not be recounted here. Francisco and Jacinta were told of their early death in their visions of Mary, and they both succumbed to the Spanish flu the next year. Normally children are not considered for canonization since they are thought to be too young to understand and practice heroic virtue. But in 1979, more than three hundred bishops asked Pope St. John Paul II to consider canonizing the children because so much good had come from the Fatima miracles. The bishops also noted that many miracles were being reported by the faithful after asking the children for their intentions. In 1979, the Congregation for the Causes of Saints started debating whether it would be appropriate to make an exception.

Two years later a would-be assassin shot Pope John Paul II four times in St. Peter's square, with one bullet barely missing his heart. The day of the attack was May 13, 1981, the anniversary of the first vision at Fatima. The pope was deeply affected by this, and one year later he said during a visit to Fatima:

> On this exact date last year in St. Peter's Square, in Rome, there was an attempt on the life of your Pope, which mysteriously coincided with the anniversary of the first vision at Fatima, that of 13 May 1917. The coincidence of these dates was so great that it seemed to be a special invitation for me to come here.[3]

In 1989, the children were declared Venerable by Pope John Paul II, and eleven years later, they were declared Blessed by the Congregation for the Causes of Saints. The search for a miracle to substantiate their canonization began.

[3] Loretta G. Seyer, "Fatima Has High Hopes for Francisco and Jacinta," *National Catholic Register*, May 16, 1999, https://www.ncregister.com/news/fatima-has-high-hopes-for-francisco-and-jacinta.

On March 3, 2013, a five-year-old Brazilian boy named Lucas Batista fell twenty feet from a window. He sustained serious brain damage to the point of losing some brain tissue and was in a coma. His parents had a great devotion to Mary under the title of Our Lady of Fatima, and they contacted a nearby Carmelite monastery to ask for prayers. The convent had relics of Francisco and Jacinta, and the nuns prayed that the children intercede for Lucas. Two days later, Lucas woke up and was able to speak, and on March 11, he was discharged from the ICU. The parents report that Lucas has been normal and healthy since, with the same personality, intelligence, and character he had before the accident. This event was studied and was declared valid on March 23, 2017. Francisco and Jacinta were canonized by Pope Francis on May 13, 2017. They are the youngest saints in the Church who did not die martyrs.

Cardinal John Henry Newman

Cardinal John Henry Newman was an English convert from Anglicanism who lived from 1801 until 1890. He was well known for his writing and poetry and was an important figure in the nineteenth-century history of England and the Church, especially in the English-speaking world.

Jack Sullivan, a sixty-one-year-old man living in Hanson, Massachusetts, was in classes to become a deacon in 2000. He began to suffer severe back and leg pain. Doctors found that a vertebra in his lower back had turned inward and was severely compressing his spinal cord. He was told that he would need surgery and that the recovery would preclude completion of his studies for the diaconate. He saw a television program calling for anyone who received a miracle in response to praying to Cardinal

Newman to report it, and he prayed: "Please, Cardinal Newman, help me to walk so that I can return to classes and be ordained."[4]

The very next morning, Jack awoke without pain, and he was able to complete his third-year classes over the next nine months—but on the last day of classes, the pain in his back and legs returned. A year later, doctors performed a laminectomy to remove some bone, which left Jack in severe pain during a recovery that was expected to last several months. A few days after the surgery, he tried to get out of bed and experienced intense pain, and he prayed to Cardinal Newman again. Jack later recounted:

> Suddenly I felt an intense heat, like an oven blast, and a strong tingling sensation throughout my whole body. I felt an indescribable sense of joy and peace, and was totally transfixed by what I believed to be God's presence.
>
> When I became aware of what was happening around me I was standing upright and I explained to the nurse that I felt no more pain.[5]

His doctor testified that the recovery was unbelievable, that he had never seen someone heal so quickly and completely. Anyone who has known a spinal stenosis patient has likely witnessed the debilitating pain the condition causes. The case was studied by the Holy See and accepted as the miracle to substantiate Cardinal Newman's beatification. Jack Sullivan was ordained a deacon in 2002.

[4] Michael Hirst, "Papal Visit: Cardinal Newman's 'Miracle Cure,'" BBC News, September 12, 2010, https://www.bbc.com/news/uk-11186584.

[5] Ibid.

It is important to note that the initial reprieve from pain that Jack received in this case did not meet the full criteria for an approved miracle because it was not lasting. But that initial healing did allow him to complete that year of classes, just as he had asked of the saint. The second healing, however, met all of the criteria: spontaneous, instantaneous, complete, lasting, and unexplainable.

Melissa Villalobos first learned of Cardinal Newman in 2000 when she saw a television show about him. Her husband brought home some holy cards of the cardinal, and she developed a strong devotion to him. In 2013, Melissa was pregnant and developed a subchorionic hematoma—bleeding and a blood clot that can detach part of the placenta, causing it to tear. This was causing continuous and significant bleeding, which can lead to death. The only treatment was bed rest, but Melissa had other children to care for. On May 15, she bled more than usual and collapsed on the bathroom floor from the blood loss. She did not have her phone, and her husband was away. She prayed: "Please, Cardinal Newman, make the bleeding stop."[6]

The bleeding stopped immediately, and Melissa was able to stand. Then, amazingly, she smelled the scent of roses filling the room, and she thanked her intercessor. There was another wave of rose scent, and Melissa knew she was cured. Later that day, she had an ultrasound that confirmed that the bleeding had stopped and that the hematoma had been healed. After the baby was born,

[6] Mary Farrow, "How a Miracle through Cardinal Newman Saved a Mother and Baby in a Dangerous Pregnancy," Catholic News Agency, October 12, 2019, https://www.catholicnewsagency.com/news/how-cardinal-newman-saved-a-mother-and-baby-in-a-dangerous-pregnancy-85875.

the case was reviewed by Fr. Ignatius Harrison, the postulator for Cardinal Newman's cause for sainthood. He met with Melissa, her husband, and her doctors. He reviewed the medical records with the doctors. The case was sent to the Holy See for further investigation. After six years of investigation, on February 13, 2019, Pope Francis signed the decree recognizing the miracle. Cardinal Newman was canonized on October 13, 2019.

Mariam Baouardy

Saint Mary of Jesus Crucified was born Mariam Baouardy in 1846 in the Holy Land, which was then under the control of the Ottoman Empire. Both of her parents died when she was young, so she lived with other family members, ultimately moving to Cairo. It was there that, at the age of twelve, she was accosted by a young man who made advances and demanded she convert to Islam. When she refused, he slashed her throat and tossed her into an alley to die.

It was there that she experienced a vision of a woman in a blue habit taking her to a grotto, where she stitched the young girl's wound and cared for her. Mariam then found herself in Heaven with Mary, the angels, and the saints. A voice told her that "her book is not yet finished," and she found herself in the grotto with the nun again. She recalled that she may have spent a month there recovering. At some point the nun said to her:

> You will never see your family again; you will go to France, where you will become a religious. You will be a child of Saint Joseph before becoming a daughter of Saint Teresa. You will receive the habit of Carmel in one house; you

> will make your profession in a second; and you will die in a third, at Bethlehem.[7]

All of this came to be. Later in her life, doctors examined the damage to her throat from the cut. They found a laceration in her trachea and in an artery in her throat—wounds that normally meant certain death. A nun at her monastery recorded:

> A celebrated doctor at Marseille, who had taken care of Mariam, had confessed that, although he was an atheist, there must be a God, for from a natural point of view, could not have lived.[8]

There were many other wonders in Mariam's life, including the stigmata in her hands and her heart, visions, ecstasies, and levitations. The cause for her canonization was started in 1927, and her heroic virtue was declared in 1981. The search for miracles was started.

A baby named Khaznet was born in April 1926 with total muscular hypotonia with severe rickets syndrome. This made her thin, weak, and unable to move. Over her first years, she failed to grow strong and was never able to stand or to walk. Her family began a novena to Mariam Baouardy in December 1929. Almost immediately, the child got to her feet and began to run, jump, and move around in a completely normal way. She never regressed, living to thirty-four years old, when she was tragically killed in a house fire. The miracle was accepted on July 9, 1983, and Mariam Baouardy was beatified five months later by Pope John Paul II.

[7] "St. Mariam (Mary) of Jesus Crucified," St. Therese Church, Alhambra, California, http://www.sttheresechurchalhambra.org/?DivisionID=20008&DepartmentID=22710.

[8] Ibid.

The second miracle for Mariam's canonization also concerned a newborn baby, this one in 2015. Emanuele was born in Taormina, Sicily, underweight with blue toenails and hands, and he could not muster the strength to cry. Doctors diagnosed him with a disorder of the blood vessels that returned blood to the heart. They tried a number of surgeries but were unable to resolve it. There was nothing left to do medically, and the baby slipped into the early stages of death, with his blood pressure dropping and the electrical activity of his brain decreasing. His parents called the Carmelite Sisters of Jerusalem and asked them to pray for Emanuele. They also affixed a relic of Mariam to their baby's bedside. That same day, there was definitive improvement, and all signs of the disorder disappeared. Medical testing came back normal, and a complete recovery was verified. This miracle was formally investigated and accepted by Pope Francis on December 7, 2014, and he canonized Mariam in May of the following year.

I have shared a first-class relic of St. Mary of Jesus Crucified with a number of people who needed healing. In each case, it helped the person when he slept with the relic on his person overnight. One person experienced a complete healing of a year-long untreatable migraine. Another person's medically unexplained chest pains ceased. A third person experienced a spiritual healing. Finally, while being used during a solemn exorcism (in which I applied it to the possessed person's head without saying what the relic was or showing it to him), the relic caused a demon immediately to rage while stamping the floor and shouting, "That nun! That nun! She is helping the Christians in the Middle East die well! She is making them saints! That nun is stealing so many souls from us! That nun! THAT NUN!"

St. Kateri Tekakwitha

Kateri Tekakwitha was born in 1656 in what is now Auriesville, New York, to Christian Algonquin parents. Smallpox took her parents and left her face disfigured and her eyes damaged. She refused to marry and, after instruction by Jesuit missionaries, she was baptized on Easter Sunday in 1676. She experienced great opposition to her faith and so made a two-hundred-mile journey to the Christian village of Saint-Louis near Montreal. Kateri grew in devotion and holiness over time, and at twenty-three she took a vow of virginity. This vow had a serious impact on her life, as her future in her culture depended on her being married. She practiced penances and extreme fasting for the conversion of her nation, all while teaching children about God and caring for the elderly. She died at twenty-four years old. The process for her canonization began in 1884, and Pope Pius XII declared her venerable in 1943. The normal requirement of a miracle for beatification was waived by Pope John Paul II, and he beatified her on June 22, 1980.

On a Saturday in 2006, five-year-old Jake Finkbonner was playing basketball when he fell and cut his lip. In the vast majority of cases this would be a simple wound, but the cut became infected with flesh-eating bacteria, and by the next day, he was severely ill. On Monday he was life-flighted to Children's Hospital in Seattle. Jake's diagnosis of necrotizing fasciitis, in which the bacteria aggressively kill off body tissue, was potentially fatal. By Tuesday, he was in critical condition, and he remained so for two weeks. The family's pastor suggested that they pray for the intercession of Blessed Kateri because she had also suffered from a disease that disfigured her face. After praying for two weeks, Jake's great aunt brought a religious sister who had taken the name Kateri to pray for Jake. Sister Kateri had a relic of Bl. Kateri, which she placed on his bed. After weeks of not responding to treatment, the infection receded that very day. The recovery was investigated by the local bishop and was submitted to the Congregation for the Causes of Saints as a potential miracle. The Congregation approved it, and Blessed Kateri was canonized on October 12, 2012, by Pope Benedict XVI.

Padre Pio

Padre Pio is one of the most famous and popular saints in the Catholic Church, in part due to his stigmata and numerous other miracles attributed to him during his lifetime. He was born in Pietrelcina, Italy, in 1887, and he died on September 23, 1968, in San Giovanni Rotondo. His cause was opened almost immediately, but it took until 1997 to conclude the evaluation of his life and writings so that he could be called Venerable. Then the search for a confirmed miracle for his beatification started.

On the first day of November 1995, Consiglia De Martino, an Italian woman with three children, experienced a rupture of her thoracic duct. This is the largest lymph vessel in the human body. Half a gallon of lymphatic fluid poured into her chest just under her left collarbone. Consiglia went to the hospital and was told that a difficult surgery was required; it was scheduled for two days later. While she was in the hospital, she called Br. Modestino da Pietrelcina, a spiritual son of Padre Pio whom she had met during visits to San Giovanni Rotondo, and asked him to pray for her to Padre Pio, whom she had met several times before his death. Br. Modestino prayed for Consiglia's healing at Padre Pio's tomb, and that very day, she smelled the "intense perfume of Padre Pio" while walking back to her room in the hospital. She had the same experience the next day—and she began to feel better.

When November 3 came, Consiglia's doctors checked her before the surgery and found that the swelling had gone away. They repeated all the necessary tests, and it was confirmed: the fluid had simply vanished and her thoracic duct had healed. The next day, she heard a voice say, "Lina, you are healed," and she smelled the same perfume of Padre Pio. On November 6, only five days after her ordeal began, she left the hospital. The healing was scrutinized and determined to be inexplicable by natural means. Pope John Paul II proclaimed Padre Pio Blessed on May 2, 1999.

The next year, Padre Pio intervened in the life of Matteo Pio Colella, a seven-year-old son of a doctor who worked at the Home for the Relief of Suffering, the charitable hospital Padre Pio had set up during his lifetime. Matteo developed a fever at school on January 20, 2000, and it advanced to over 104 degrees by that evening. The boy soon went into septic shock and into a coma; doctors had to put him on a respirator. His heart stopped, but doctors revived him. At this point, the prognosis was not good: Matteo was near death. Septic shock results when an infection enters the bloodstream and causes a drop in blood pressure, which is very dangerous. It can be difficult to get septic infections under control, and it usually takes significant time to do so. Since the infection had stopped Matteo's heart once, it was unlikely that they could cure him before it happened again.

Matteo's mother, Lucia, went to pray a Rosary at the tomb of Padre Pio. While praying there with her eyes closed, she saw a vision of Padre Pio lifting her son from his bed and helping him to stand. In the same place, three days later, she experienced a strong scent of flowers. Less than a week after that, Matteo came out of his coma. He told his mother that while he was asleep, he saw himself lying on the bed from a distance, and he saw an old man with a white beard and a brown habit. This man took his hand and said, "Matteo, don't worry, you will get well quickly." Doctors ordered a CAT scan that found no indication of any damage in his body. The healing was studied locally in the diocese, and then by the Congregation for the Causes of Saints. Padre Pio was canonized on June 16, 2002, by Pope John Paul II.

In solemn exorcisms, we often use relics of various saints or relics of the Passion of Jesus. Sometimes we have relics that come to us from reliable people but without paperwork. Though testing relics during exorcisms is in no way definitive, it can be interesting to see whether they cause reactions. Sometimes we test them by applying them during the exorcism rite, and sometimes we ask the people if they feel anything before the exorcism starts, while they are in their normal, human state of mind.

A priest friend had been allowed to examine one of Padre Pio's gloves, and he saw in its fabric a white hair that may have come from the saint. With permission, he kept the hair and put it in a sealed plastic bag. He brought this possible relic to one of our sessions, a case we were completely certain was a legitimate possession. I asked the person before the session if he would hold the bag and see if he felt something. I did not tell him what was in the bag, and the tiny hair was not discernible in the bag. Immediately after taking the bag, he doubled over and let out a shriek of pain while holding his head with his other hand. His hand holding the bag started to shake uncontrollably as he moaned in pain.

I asked him what he was feeling, and he responded that he felt an intense pain in his head as soon as he touched the bag—as if his brain were splitting in two. I asked if he could tell me anything about who the bag was connected with. After some moments, he said it was an old man. I asked what color clothing this man was wearing. He said brown. I asked if he had a sense of who the man was. After a long pause, he said he was embarrassed and that he was sure he was wrong, but was it Padre Pio? When the solemn exorcism was in progress, I used the relic again, and it again elicited a painful reaction from the demon, just as we see with other confirmed relics. Since this hair had no documentation and was not in a theca (a small metal container with a glass window made to hold relics) with a proper wax seal, however, it cannot be used in public veneration.

Thérèse of Lisieux

Thérèse, due to her humble simplicity and the many miracles attributed to her since her death, is another of the most beloved and well-known saints in the world. She was born in 1873 in Alençon, France, entered the Carmelite monastery at age fifteen (with special permission from the pope), and lived a hidden, simple life of prayer. At the urging of her superior, she wrote her famous autobiography, *The Story of a Soul*, in which she described her "little way" of spirituality. She promised to spend her eternity in Heaven doing good deeds on earth, and to "let fall a shower of roses."[9] After a painful time of illness she died of tuberculosis on September 30, 1897, at the age of twenty-four.

The cause for Thérèse's canonization started soon after, on June 10, 1914. This was unusually soon after her death, but

[9] *Story of a Soul: The Autobiography of St. Thérèse of Lisieux*, ed. Rev. T.N. Taylor (London: Burns, Oates & Washbourne, 1922), epilogue, Christian Classics Ethereal Library, https://www.ccel.org/ccel/therese/autobio.toc.html.

such was the great love and admiration she had inspired in the hearts of so many. The study of her life and writings was complete by August 14, 1921, when she was declared Venerable by Benedict XV.

The first miracle that was approved was the healing of Sr. Louise of St. Germain, who was cured of stomach ulcers that she had suffered for three years. Sr. Louise prayed to Thérèse, and on the night of September 10, 1916, the saint appeared to her and said she would recover soon. The other nuns found rose petals of various colors on the bed of Sr. Louise the next morning. A few days later, Sr. Louise awoke completely healed. X-rays and doctors' certifications confirmed the authenticity of the healing.

The second miracle was the healing of Charles Anne, a young seminarian who was dying from advanced pulmonary tuberculosis. During the night, he felt that he was dying, and the young man prayed to Thérèse for her intervention with God. The examining doctor testified:

> The destroyed and ravaged lungs have been replaced by new lungs, carrying out their normal functions and about to revive the entire organism. A slight emaciation persists, which will disappear within a few days under a regularly assimilated diet.[10]

Charles Anne went on to be ordained a priest, and he witnessed Thérèse's beatification on April 29, 1923. At this time, the Church required two miracles for beatification and two more

[10] "Frequently Asked Questions about St. Thérèse," Society of the Little Flower, https://www.littleflower.org/therese/st-therese-faqs/#what-are-the-four-miracles-that-made-therese-a-sai.

for canonization, so there was more work to be done. The two miracles for Thérèse's canonization, like the second for her beatification, involved tuberculosis—the illness that she had suffered with during her life.

That year, Sr. Gabrielle of the Poor Daughters of the Sacred Heart in Parma, Italy, developed a lesion on her knee from repeatedly breaking firewood. This became infected with tuberculosis and resisted treatment. The infection ate away at the bone and then spread to her spine. The knee lesion made it impossible for her to kneel without great pain, and the spinal lesion required her to wear a back brace. After all attempts at treatment failed, a priest suggested that she go to a prayer service in honor of Thérèse. That night, after the prayer service, she knelt for prayer in the chapel and did not feel any pain in her knee. Later that evening, she took off her back brace and declared that she was cured. She returned to the work of her religious life without difficulties. The healing was scrutinized by doctors and deemed to be miraculous.

Marie Pellemans of Schaerbeek, Belgium, was the recipient of the final cure attributed to Thérèse for her canonization. She had contracted pulmonary tuberculosis, and it spread to her intestines. She went to Lourdes in 1920 to seek a cure, but without success. In 1923, she visited the town of Lisieux and knelt at the tomb of Thérèse, where she was suddenly restored to perfect health. The doctor who had diagnosed her, Dr. Vandensteene, said:

> I found Miss Pellemans literally transformed. This young woman, previously out of breath from the least movement, now moves about without fatigue; she eats everything given to her, with a very good appetite. The abdomen presents no tender point, when formerly the

> least pressure produced severe pain. All symptoms of tubercular ulceration of the intestine have disappeared.[11]

Thérèse was canonized on May 17, 1925—fewer than thirty years after her death—by Pope Pius XI.

In 2007, I was helping with exorcisms in a diocese that had a Carmelite monastery of nuns dedicated to Thérèse. Sometimes before the exorcisms we would go to Benediction at the monastery. After Benediction, the priest would hold a bone of Thérèse sealed in a reliquary for veneration. The people would line up, kiss the relic, and file out of the chapel. I had done this many times before.

On this day when I kissed the reliquary, I felt a strong electrical shock, like when your finger is zapped by a doorknob after walking on a carpet. In this case, though, there was no carpet in the stone chapel and the reliquary cover was made of glass. The sting was strong, and I was briefly unconscious. I came to while falling sideways and caught myself before I hit the floor. The priest looked surprised and concerned as I slowly returned to my pew, a bit dizzy. As I sat, I experienced several religious visions of myself in ministry, and I felt the strong presence of Thérèse. After about five minutes, this state faded, and I was able to get up and leave normally.

I wrote to the Mother Superior of the Carmel to tell her what had happened and to ask for any guidance she might have. She wrote back that many supernatural events have happened with relics of Thérèse and that my experience was not unusual. This never happened again in future visits to the chapel, but it left an impression on me that even now I do not fully understand.

[11] Ibid.

Conclusions

Miraculous healings were important in the time of Jesus, and they are important now. God's meeting our needs in a special way is not only something we hope for personally but something we want to hear about. Even *hearing about* a healing comforts us and gives us hope, often more so than other types of miracles. The alleviation of suffering demonstrates not just that God is real, but that He loves and cares for us.

But what determines who gets chosen to be healed? During the investigation of the causes of saints there is a global call for miracles, and millions around the world pray for them. Only a handful are verified and publicized, and likely some other legitimate healings are not made public because they were not chosen to substantiate a cause. The shrine at Lourdes, which we will consider in the next chapter, gives us a sense of numbers. About six million people visit the shrine per year, and there have been between 60 and 70 verified healings since 1858. Even if only 30 percent of the visitors are seeking healing and the rest are family and friends, that amounts to 291 million people who prayed there for a healing since 1858. That is a verified miraculous healing rate of about 0.0000002 percent. Is this reflective of God's limited activity, or are there other factors?

Recall that Thomas Aquinas first defined miracles as things we cannot explain. The healings we *can* explain have certainly increased as science has progressed, and many events once considered miraculous are no longer so considered. Aquinas then described three orders of miracles: things that nature cannot do (raising the dead), things that nature can do but in a different order (restoring sight to those born blind), and things that nature does but at a different speed (curing an infection and fever instantly instead of over days). The Church sets the bar for a healing to be declared miraculous very high in order to separate acts of God from nature *conclusively*, but does God operate only in this extreme? Is God limited to acting only in the ways we define? We will never know in this life how many times God intervened more subtly in the sufferings of the praying faithful, in ways that don't fit the Church's stringent but prudent criteria but were still truly miraculous.

The idea of praying for a healing is all but universal. When we cease to feel in control of our lives, we appeal to God to regain something like control through Him. If we can make God do our will, then things will be safe again. But I think the universality of this kind of prayer has another explanation: on some level, we know that healings are more common than the one-in-a-million verified miracles at Lourdes. I know that I am not alone in having heard many stories of prayer saving a person's life or alleviating suffering. These stories may not pass rigorous scientific muster, but God is not limited by science, and not everything that is "explainable" by science happened through purely natural means. I think that God's healings are numerous, but most are never heard of. Millions may have been healed in a quiet way.

I have a priest friend who does expositions of holy relics, including a large relic of the true Cross. He has thousands of e-mails from people claiming to have been healed after touching the relics. Many have sent in medical verification. That is only one priest's ministry: How many other quiet healings have occurred?

Jesus came not to ignore our pleas but, as He said, that we "may have life and have it abundantly" (John 10:10).

3

Apparitions of Mary

The first apparition of Mary happened in the year 40, when Mary was still alive. She was living in Jerusalem and appeared to the apostle James the Greater in Spain. The apparition was controversial in Spain but was later approved by the Congregation of Rites in 1723 under Pope Innocent XIII. This first apparition was really a bilocation since Mary was physically present in Jerusalem when she appeared in Spain. The supernatural aspects of the account were described in the book *The Mystical City of God* by the Venerable Mary of Agreda in 1665.[12]

Marian apparitions generally include four components: the visionary, the experience, the message, and the miracles. But within this framework, there has been a wide variety. The visionaries are sometimes children, sometimes professed religious, and sometimes lay adults. The experiences all include Our Lady, but sometimes she appears in her fullness, other times merely as a voice, and still other times as a statue or image that moves or speaks. The messages are almost always centered on prayer and repentance, but sometimes they include dire warnings for the

[12] Venerable Mary of Agreda, *The Mystical City of God*, 4 vols. (Charlotte, NC: TAN Books, 2009).

world. The accompanying miracles vary widely, from enduring images to one-time spectacles, but they are almost always testable by outside experts, so the Church and the world have some proof that something extraordinary happened.

Once a report of such an event is made—or an ongoing event is noticed—the local bishop makes two important determinations. First, he discerns whether the messages connected with the apparition are in accord with the Catholic Faith. Of course, if they are not, it means the event is a fraud, either human or demonic. Second, he investigates whether any aspects of the event were miraculous in nature. The pope may later endorse the event through some recognition, such as consecrating a shrine, but it is not the pope who approves or disapproves apparitions or their messages. In practice, though, the local bishop usually works in cooperation with Rome because most bishops are unsure of exactly how to investigate such extraordinary happenings.

Apparitions and messages of any kind are always considered private revelation, even if they are approved by the local bishop. This means that Catholics are never required to believe them or even to pay attention to them. That being said, these messages and events have had huge impacts on the world—their locations becoming sites of pilgrimage for millions and causing healings and conversions for centuries.

What most people do not know is that, although only a handful of apparitions have been officially approved—ten by local bishops and sixteen by Rome in some way—there have been hundreds of accounts of Marian apparitions down through the centuries. Sometimes the supposed apparitions generated some local interest, but no investigation was undertaken; sometimes there has been disagreement between diocesan and Vatican authorities. The ongoing case of Medjugorje, Bosnia-Herzegovina, from 1981 to today is a complicated version of this latter case. As of 2020, Rome has approved pilgrimages to the site, but final full approval has been withheld until the apparent visions conclude and the case can be studied in its entirety.

Our Lady of Guadalupe (1531)

Only a decade after Spanish conquistadors defeated the Aztec Empire and established Spanish rule in 1519, one of the most famous events in Christendom occurred. Juan Diego was a poor uneducated man who had left Aztec paganism for Christianity. He lived near a hill named Tepeyac, which had been consecrated to an Aztec goddess and where special devotions occurred every year on December 12. On December 12, 1531, Juan Diego saw a very different Lady on Tepeyac: the Virgin Mary. She announced that she was "the mother of the true God who gives life." She asked that a church be built on Tepeyac in her honor. Juan Diego sought out the archbishop of Mexico City, Fray Juan de Zumárraga and reported the apparition to him, but the bishop did not believe him. Mary appeared a second time at the hill and told Juan Diego to continue insisting on her requests to the bishop.

The bishop then told Juan Diego to go back to the Lady on Tepeyac Hill and ask for proof that she was who she claimed to be. Juan Diego did so, and Mary told him she would comply with the bishop's request the next day. On that day, Juan Diego's uncle was very ill, seemingly near death, and Juan Diego felt that he had to attend to him rather than to go Our Lady. He tried to avoid Tepeyac on his way to find a priest for his uncle, but Mary appeared to him anyway. She assured Juan Diego that his uncle would be cured, saying, "Am I not here, I who am your mother?" These words are over the door to the shrine of Our Lady of Guadalupe today.

Mary told Juan Diego to gather flowers from the hill—flowers that should not have been blooming in wintertime. She arranged the flowers in his tilma, or cloak, to be delivered to the bishop. When Juan Diego did so, Zumárraga was not only amazed by the roses. He, and all present, saw an incredibly beautiful image of Mary on the fabric of the tilma. This was the miraculous sign the bishop had asked for.

This tilma has become world famous. It is one of the most recognizable images of Our Lady and has led to the conversion of millions of people, especially in South America. The image is a symbol of national unity and pride for Mexicans and many other Latin Americans. Mary appears as a Mestiza woman in the image, reminding us of her universal motherhood. The tilma is sixty-seven inches high and forty-one inches wide and has been studied several times through the centuries—not without criticism and controversy. It is likely that the tilma will continue to be debated, attacked, and defended. There have been debates about whether the image was painted, whether it was retouched during the communist Mexican revolution of the 1910s, whether it is on cactus fibers or hemp, and whether people can be seen reflected in the eyes of the image.

It is perhaps somewhat misguided to invest so heavily in whether the tilma is miraculous. It is an image, like all icons, of a spiritual reality. It points to that reality and is a window to it for the viewer, but it is not the reality itself. It would certainly be compelling if it were of miraculous origin, but that would not solely validate God or the Church. If it did so, that would be too great an emphasis on one object.

In 1895, Pope Leo XIII granted the tilma image a canonical coronation, which is an official recognition from the Vatican for the image and its related devotions. In 2002, Pope John Paul II canonized Juan Diego in Mexico City, further cementing the Vatican's opinion of the case. The tilma continues to be on display in the Basilica of Guadalupe in Mexico City.

Our Lady of the Miraculous Medal (1830)

Catherine Labouré was born in France in 1806, in the immediate aftermath of the French Revolution. A great persecution of the Church occurred during the revolution, and France became officially a godless nation. Napoleon had seized power in 1799, and during his rule, there were some attempts to reestablish relations with Pope Pius VII, but these faltered and failed. The Napoleonic Wars served, in part, to spread the new liberal-secular ideals of France across Europe by force, and the era of the social-political power of the Church that had begun in the Middle Ages came to a conclusion. The emperor kept the Holy Father under house arrest from 1809 to 1814, but Napoleon was finally defeated in 1815. It was at this critical moment—as in 1531 in Mexico—that Mary intervened. The following story and quotes are taken from the Association of the Miraculous Medal.

When Catherine's mother died in 1815, the young girl turned to the Virgin Mary to be her mother. Three years later, at the age of twelve, she had a dream about a priest who beckoned her to follow him, but she withdrew. Later she had another dream in which the same priest came to her and said:

> My child, it is a good deed to look after the sick; you run away now, but one day you will be glad to come to me. God has designs on you—do not forget it.

Later, while visiting a hospital run by the Daughters of Charity, Catherine saw on the wall a picture of the priest from her dreams. It was St. Vincent de Paul, the founder of the hospital's order. Two years later, in 1830, Catherine joined the Daughters of Charity.

That same year, on July 19, she was awakened during the night by a bright light and the voice of a child, who said, "Sr. Labouré, come to the Chapel; the Blessed Virgin awaits you." The novice went to the chapel and found it lit as if for midnight Mass. She knelt at the Communion rail and prayed, then heard the rustle of fabric and saw the Virgin Mary enter the chapel and sit down. The Blessed Mother said:

> God wishes to charge you with a mission. You will be contradicted, but do not fear; you will have the grace to do what is necessary. Tell your spiritual director all that passes within you. Times are evil in France and in the world. Come to the foot of the altar. Graces will be shed on all, great and little, especially upon those who ask for them. You will have the protection of God and Saint Vincent. I always will have my eyes upon you. There will be much persecution. The cross will be treated with contempt. It will be hurled to the ground and blood will flow.

Sr. Catherine lived the normal life of a novice after this visitation until November 27 of that year. During evening meditation in the chapel, all the members of the house were there praying. Sister then heard the same sound of Mary's clothing and looked up. She saw Mary standing on a globe, and Mary spoke:

> Have a medal struck after this model. All who wear it will receive great graces; they should wear it around the neck. Graces will abound for persons who wear it with confidence.

Sr. Catherine asked how she was to accomplish this task. Mary told her to go to her confessor, saying that he was to be Mary's servant. It took two years of convincing, but eventually he came to believe her and went to the archbishop, who ordered two thousand medals to be made. It is important to note that the identity of Sr. Catherine was not revealed to anyone except her confessor, and her order had no idea that she had seen Mary.

By 1836, the medal had become popular and was becoming associated with miraculous healings across Europe. Rosalie Ducas, a five-year-old girl in Belgium, had lost her sight the previous year. Her mother put a miraculous medal around her neck and started a novena to Mary, asking for her healing. Within six hours of wearing the medal, Rosalie stopped feeling the pain she had felt since losing her sight. After a few days of the novena, she opened her eyes, and by the end of the novena her sight had been completely restored. There were many such stories, causing the medal to become more and more popular.

Sr. Catherine went on to live more than forty years of quiet service to the elderly and the sick. In 1876, she knew that she would die within that year. Mary told her that she was now to tell her superior about her visions all those years ago. On the last day of 1876, Sr. Catherine died. When the cause of her sainthood was being investigated in 1933, authorities exhumed her body and found it intact and supple, her eyes visibly blue. It was fifty-seven years after death, and there was no modern embalming. Her body is still visible under a side altar of the Chapel of the Apparition in Paris.

The miraculous medal did not stop producing miracles in the 1800s. In 1943, Claude Newman, a death-row inmate, was given a miraculous medal. The Blessed Mother appeared to him and told him that she would be his mother if he would confess his sins to a priest and get baptized. He went to confession and shared the great forgiveness he found in the sacrament with other inmates. Mary appeared to him again and told him of a private vow the priest had made to her: that he would build a church in her honor if the priest survived a life-threatening situation. Claude reported this to the priest, and combined with his conversion, it confirmed to the priest that Claude's visions were real. As Claude waited for execution, he prayed for another inmate who hated religion and hated Claude. When the time for his execution came, Claude was happy, even celebratory, because he was going to Heaven. After Claude's death, when the other inmate's execution date came, he became overwhelmed by fear. He had received a vision of Claude and Mary, who showed him a vision of Hell. He called for a priest and was absolved, returning to his faith. The miraculous medal was instrumental in Mary's intervention to save these souls.

Our Lady of Lourdes (1858)

Bernadette Soubirous was a fourteen-year-old peasant girl in Lourdes, France, in 1858. On February 11, she was gathering firewood near a rock face with her sister Toinette and their friend Jeanne Abadie. Suddenly she heard the sound of wind and then, looking at a small indentation in the rock, she saw Our Lady as a small young woman. Toinette and Jeanne did not see Mary, but they saw Bernadette go into an ecstasy—a kind of a spiritual trance. The young visionary was initially scared, but Mary gently invited her to pray the Rosary with her.

Bernadette wanted to keep the event secret, but her sister told their mother that evening. On her next trip to the site, she brought holy water and threw it at the image in order to dispel the fear that it was a deception from the devil. Bernadette told the image of Mary that if she did indeed come from God, she should stay, but if not then she should go. Mary just bowed her head and stayed. There was no particular message at this second apparition. On a third visit, the apparition asked her for prayer and penance for the conversion of sinners.

The next day Bernadette returned yet again. This time Mary directed her to dig at a particular spot and drink from the water she would find there. She indeed found a spring, which continues to flow to this day. Miracles started happening to people who drank from this spring: ailing people would be healed and cured. The idea of healing springs has been common since biblical times, but they were often hoaxes. The local government, skeptical of the notoriety of the place, fenced off the area from the public. But only a few months later, in October 1858, Emperor Napoleon III himself ordered the grotto reopened. The place had become a national issue in just eight months.

The most famous part of the message of Our Lady of Lourdes came during the time the grotto was closed. Bernadette sneaked in during the night, and Mary appeared to her and said, "I am the Immaculate Conception." The Dogma of the Immaculate Conception—that Mary was free from original sin from the moment of her conception—had just been declared by Pope Pius IX in 1854, four years earlier.

The Church did a formal investigation of the case from November 17, 1858, until January 18, 1860. On the final day, Bishop Bertrand Severt Laurence declared:

> We are inspired by the Commission comprising wise, holy, learned and experienced priests who questioned the child, studied the facts, examined everything and weighed all

> the evidence. We have also called on science, and we remain convinced that the Apparitions are supernatural and divine, and that by consequence, what Soubirous saw was the Most Blessed Virgin. Our convictions are based on the testimony of Soubirous, but above all on the things that have happened, things which can be nothing other than divine intervention.

Since then, Lourdes has become one of the most visited Marian shrines in the world, with four to six million visitors each year.

Though there have been many conversions at Lourdes, it is most famous for medical healings, claims of which are so numerous that there is a permanent Office of Medical Observations on site to study them. People who believe they have been cured can present their case right there and start the investigation process.

A century ago, many disease mechanisms, including spontaneous remission, were poorly understood, and treatment options were far fewer. As time has gone on, we have been able to explain more and more healing miracles, and fewer have been reported and confirmed by the Church's strict criteria. Out of about six million people who visit Lourdes each year, only about forty claim to have been miraculously healed—and most of these cases are not validated by the doctors. Between sixty and seventy healings at Lourdes have been declared miraculous since 1858.

Bernadette Soubirous, like many other visionaries, was eventually canonized. She took the habit of the Sisters of Charity but was sickly throughout her life. She died in 1879 at the age of thirty-five and was declared a saint in 1933 by Pope Pius XI.

Our Lady of Fatima (1917)

The Marian apparitions at Fatima, Portugal, are probably the most famous of the Marian apparitions. This is because they include arguably the most dramatic miracle since biblical times, a secret message, and prophecies about the coming Second World War. They addressed secular politics directly and have become a rallying point for ideological movements in the Church. Fatima was also addressed and confirmed years later in the approved apparitions of Mary in Akita, Japan, in 1973.

The visions and messages of Fatima came during the greatest mass loss of human life up to that point in history, World War I. Total casualties of the war were around twenty million. The primary message of Fatima was to pray for sinners who would die and go to Hell if no one prayed for them. In that sense, the Fatima apparitions were a loving action of God to help those millions of souls through the intervention of His mother and His angel.

Three poor, illiterate shepherd children were herding sheep near their village of Aljustrel in 1916: Lucia Santos and her cousins Francisco Marto and Jacinta Marto. Lucia was nine, Francisco was eight, and Jacinta was six. Three times that year, they were visited by an angel who said he was the "Angel of Peace" and the "Guardian Angel of Portugal." St. Michael the Archangel had been known as the "Angel of Peace" by the Church for centuries by that time, reflected in the Liturgy of the Hours, the breviary, hymns of the Church, and an ancient Litany of St. Michael. St. Michael taught the children prayers to say, how to make sacrifices for the sins of others, and to spend time in adoration of Jesus in the Eucharist. It seems likely that this spiritual formation was to help prepare the children for the experiences they would have the next year. The children did not tell anyone about meeting this angel until later.

In the spring of 1917, there were more visits from St. Michael in the fields, and then, in May 1917, the children met a wondrous lady there who radiated light "brighter than the sun." The lady asked the children to devote themselves to the Blessed Trinity. She also asked them to pray the Rosary every day to bring peace and an end to the Great War. Mary also implored the children to pray for sinners so that they would not go to Hell, saying that many souls go to Hell because there is no one to pray for them. Lucia said they should keep this secret, as they had the angel's appearances, but Jacinta told her disbelieving mother. Within a day, the whole village knew.

Mary had promised a miracle at her last apparition on October 13, 1917. She also promised to reveal who she was. (The children knew her as "the lady.") There had been considerable media coverage of the events in Fatima with the children, and word had spread about this promised miracle, though nobody knew what it might be.

Somewhere between thirty thousand and one hundred thousand people gathered on the appointed day, hoping to see a miracle. There were photographers, reporters, believers, and atheists. What has become known as "the miracle of the sun" occurred. A number of books have been written on the event, and many firsthand accounts were recorded, including in the papers of the time. First, here is a quote from the Portuguese newspaper O *Século*, written by the reporter Avelino de Almeida:

> Before the astonished eyes of the people, whose attitude carries us back to biblical times and who, full of terror, heads uncovered, gaze into the blue of the sky, the

> sun has trembled, and the sun has made some brusque movements, unprecedented and outside of all cosmic laws—the sun has "danced," according to the typical expression of the peasants.
>
> The people ask one another if they have seen anything and what they have seen. The greatest number avow that they have seen the trembling and dancing of the sun. Others, however, declare that they have seen the smiling face of the Virgin herself; swear that the sun turned around itself like a wheel of fireworks; that it fell, almost to the point of burning the earth with its rays.... Another tells that he has seen it change color successively.[13]

Alfredo da Silva Santos was present and reported the following:

> The sun began to move and at a certain moment appeared to us to be detached from the sky and about to hurtle upon us like a wheel of flame. My wife ... fainted, and I was too upset to attend to her.... I fell on my knees oblivious of everything and when I got up I don't know what I said. I think I began to cry out like the others. An old man with a white beard began to attack the atheists aloud and challenged them to say whether or not something supernatural had occurred.[14]

Bishop of Leiria José Alves Correia da Silva wrote a pastoral letter on the event, which included the following:

[13] "The Final Apparition," Salve Maria Regina, http://www.salvemariaregina.info/Reference/Oct13th.html.

[14] "Sixth Apparition of Our Lady," 100 Years of Fatima, https://www.ewtn.com/fatima/sixth-apparition-of-our-lady.asp.

> This phenomenon, which was not registered in any astronomical observatory, and could not therefore, have been of natural origin, was witnessed by people of every category and class, by believers as well as unbelievers, journalists of the principal daily papers and even by people kilometers away, a fact which destroys any theory of collective hallucinations.[15]

In October 1930, the bishop of that diocese declared the visions of Fatima as "worthy of belief." Francisco and Jacinta were canonized by Pope Francis on May 13, 2017.

May 13, 1981, was the anniversary of the first appearance of Mary to the children at Fatima. On this day, there was an assassination attempt on Pope St. John Paul II. He developed a stronger interest in Fatima after this and visited the site a year later, then again on the tenth anniversary of the attempt, and then again on the Great Jubilee of the Church in 2000.

Our Lady of Akita (1973)

Sr. Agnes Sasagawa was born seriously premature on May 28, 1931, and subsequently had many health problems throughout her life, including a botched operation that immobilized her for over a decade. Her health improved, though, after she drank some water from Lourdes. Later her struggles continued, and she went totally deaf. It was in this condition that she joined the Handmaids of the Holy Eucharist near Akita, Japan.

[15] Father John de Marchi, I.M.C., *The True Story of Fatima*, chap. 10, "6th Apparition of Mary—October 13th," posted on EWTN, https://www.ewtn.com/catholicism/library/true-story-of-fatima-5915.

In 1973, Sr. Agnes experienced stigmata on her left palm in the shape of a small cross, which she showed to her mother superior. This wound would follow a weekly pattern: it would swell on Thursdays, bleed on Fridays, and heal to a scar on Saturdays.

Then overnight on July 6, 1973, an angel brought her to the chapel and told her that a similar wound had developed on the statue of Mary in the chapel. This was a wooden statue standing in front of a cross with her hands open to the viewer at her sides. The statue then spoke to the sister:

> My daughter, my novice, you have obeyed me well in abandoning all to follow me. Is the infirmity of your ears painful? Your deafness will be healed, be sure. Does the wound of your hand cause you to suffer? Pray in reparation for the sins of men. Each person in this community is my irreplaceable daughter. Do you say well the prayer of the Handmaids of the Eucharist? Then, let us pray it together.[16]

The mother superior and the other nuns confirmed that the wounds on Sr. Agnes's hand and those on the statue's hand were identically shaped. Further, over the course of six years, the statue wept more than one hundred times, and after each instance, the wounds would temporarily disappear. The weeping was so visible and obvious that on a few occasions, it was broadcast on Japanese national television.

The statue ultimately gave two more messages to Sr. Agnes. One was a straightforward call to repentance and penance:

[16] Quoted in John Ata, "A Message from Our Lady—Akita, Japan," message of July 6, 1973, EWTN, https://www.ewtn.com/catholicism/library/message-from-our-lady--akita-japan-5167.

> Many men in this world afflict the Lord. I desire souls to console Him to soften the anger of the Heavenly Father. I wish, with my Son, for souls who will repair by their suffering and their poverty for the sinners and ingrates.[17]

The other, delivered on October 13, 1973—the same date Mary had appeared at Fatima—was more dire:

> My dear daughter, listen well to what I have to say to you. You will inform your superior.
>
> As I told you, if men do not repent and better themselves, the Father will inflict a terrible punishment on all humanity. It will be a punishment greater than the deluge, such as one will never seen before. Fire will fall from the sky and will wipe out a great part of humanity, the good as well as the bad, sparing neither priests nor faithful. The survivors will find themselves so desolate that they will envy the dead. The only arms which will remain for you will be the Rosary and the Sign left by My Son. Each day recite the prayers of the Rosary. With the Rosary, pray for the Pope, the bishops and priests.
>
> The work of the devil will infiltrate even into the Church in such a way that one will see cardinals opposing cardinals, bishops against bishops. The priests who venerate me will be scorned and opposed by their confreres... churches and altars sacked; the Church will be full of those who accept compromises and the demon will press many priests and consecrated souls to leave the service of the Lord.

[17] Quoted in ibid., message of August 3, 1973.

> The demon will be especially implacable against souls consecrated to God. The thought of the loss of so many souls is the cause of my sadness. If sins increase in number and gravity, there will be no longer pardon for them.
>
> With courage, speak to your superior. He will know how to encourage each one of you to pray and to accomplish works of reparation.[18]

Bishop John Shojiro Ito of the Diocese of Niigata, where Akita is located, consulted with Rome about the case, and it remained under investigation for eight years. Bishop Ito eventually released a statement indicating that he found in the messages nothing contrary to the Faith and that the events related to the statue were indeed supernatural. Since these statements have not been reversed by his successors or the Vatican, they remain in force.

The final message from Mary to Sr. Agnes may be reasonably disturbing to some. We must first remember that these are private revelations, and therefore there is no requirement to believe them or take them seriously. That being said, we should not simply dismiss any message we find uncomfortable, especially when it is repeated over multiple events. Messages in Marian apparitions always call for prayer and conversion, and often warn of future troubles. They are challenging in both cases.

The Church has had many difficult times through her history, and there have been many times of internal conflict. The more important fact is that the Church has survived, which is an indication that it is the Church Jesus founded and declared that He would not abandon.

[18] Quoted in ibid., message of October 13, 1973.

Apparition of Mary in Cairo

Mary has not only appeared at Catholic sites through history, but those are the only ones formally examined by the local bishops. There was a notable apparition of Mary at a Coptic Orthodox site in Egypt that brought about the conversion of many people and was highly documented in the modern media.

From April 2, 1968, until 1971 a glowing apparition of Mary appeared over St. Mary's Coptic Church in Zeitoun, a district of Cairo, two to three times a week. The images lasted from a few minutes to, in one case, nine hours. This is the church that tradition says is built on the site where the Holy Family stayed in Egypt. The head of the Coptic church declared that it was a genuine miracle and that the image was of Mary. Pope Paul VI sent a Vatican group to witness the miracle in person, and this is their formal statement:

> The apparitions occurred on many different nights and are continuing in different forms. The Holy Virgin Saint Mary appeared sometimes in full form and sometimes in a bust, surrounded with a halo of shining light. She was seen at times on the openings of the domes on the roof of the church, and at other times outside the domes, moving and walking on the roof of the church and over the domes. When She knelt in reverence in front of the cross, the cross shone with bright light. Waving Her blessed hands and nodding Her holy head, She blessed the people who gathered to observe the miracle. She appeared sometimes in the form of a body like a very bright cloud, and sometimes as a figure of light preceded with heavenly bodies shaped like doves moving at high speeds. The apparitions

> continued for long periods, up to 2 hours and 15 minutes as in the dawn of Tuesday April 30, 1968 (the 22nd of Barmouda, 1684 A.M.), when She appeared continuously from 2:45 am till 5:00 am.
>
> Thousands of people from different denominations and religions, Egyptians and foreign visitors, clergy and scientists, from different classes and professions, all observed the apparitions. The description of each apparition as of the time, location and configuration was identically witnessed by all people, which makes this apparition unique and sublime.[19]

More than a million people saw the apparitions in person. Many pictures and videos were recorded, and many saw it on television in Egypt. Videos taken at the time can still be seen online. The international media was generally unresponsive, though, so most of the world did not see any images or video until the events had stopped. Though there were no messages from Mary, and there were no particular visionaries, Mary caused a great strengthening of the Christian faith as well as many conversions to Christianity.

The Egyptian government and scientists tried to debunk or explain away the apparitions, and the police searched a fifteen-mile radius for projecting devices. None were found; in fact, no natural explanations of any kind were ever found.

[19] "The Apparitions of the Blessed Holy Virgin Mary to Millions in the Coptic Orthodox Church Named after Her, in Zeitoun, Cairo, Egypt (1968–1970)," The Holy Bible Web Site, https://zeitun-eg.org/zeitoun1.htm.

Conclusions

Jesus seems to prefer to speak to the world through His Mother since He went to sit next to the Father in Heaven. The messages she gives are always of prayer and conversion to her Son, and sometimes of warning if we do not do so. Mary also seems to appear at pivotal moments in history to help guide humanity to the best possible path. She has a motherly concern for us and does not want us to be lost to her and to God.

Mary intervenes for us in our earthly struggles. She tells us to avoid sin, to repent, to pray, and to avoid damnation. She talks about the ongoing choices we face and the consequences of our actions. The Christian story is not over. We cannot sit back and just wait for Heaven to be handed to us; we must struggle and fight the good fight. The Marian messages are repeated warnings and encouragement to make the right choices, to win the prize, and to attain the promise.

Let us pray.

> O God, who gave joy to the world through the Resurrection of Thy Son, our Lord Jesus Christ, grant we beseech Thee, that through the intercession of the Virgin Mary, His Mother, we may obtain the joys of everlasting life. Through the same Christ our Lord. Amen.

4

St. Michael

The Catholic Church recognizes three named archangels. Gabriel, herald of the Incarnation, appeared to Mary at the Annunciation. Raphael, missionary of healing, appears in the book of Tobit. And the most famous of all is Michael, leader of the armies of the Lord who cast Satan out of Heaven.

Michael is mentioned five times in Holy Scripture: three in the book of Daniel, one in the letter of Jude, and one in the book of Revelation. In the tenth chapter of Daniel, the prophet encounters in a dream another angel, who informs him that Michael is the protector of Israel:

> But then a hand touched me, raising me to my hands and knees.
>
> "Daniel, beloved," he said to me, "understand the words which I am speaking to you; stand up, for my mission now is to you." When he said this to me, I stood up trembling.
>
> "Do not fear, Daniel," he continued; "from the first day you made up your mind to acquire understanding and humble yourself before God, your prayer was heard. Because of it I started out, but the prince of the kingdom of Persia

> stood in my way for twenty-one days, until finally Michael, one of the chief princes, came to help me. I left him there with the prince of the kingdom of Persia, and came to make you understand what shall happen to your people in the last days; for there is yet a vision concerning those days."
>
> While he was speaking thus to me, I fell forward and kept silent.
>
> Then something like a hand touched my lips; I opened my mouth and said to the one standing before me, "My lord, I was seized with pangs at the vision and I was powerless. How can my lord's servant speak with you, my lord? For now no strength or even breath is left in me."
>
> The one who looked like a man touched me again and strengthened me, saying, "Do not fear, beloved. Peace! Take courage and be strong." When he spoke to me, I grew strong and said, "Speak, my lord, for you have strengthened me."
>
> "Do you know," he asked, "why I have come to you? Soon I must fight the prince of Persia again. When I leave, the prince of Greece will come; but I shall tell you what is written in the book of truth. No one supports me against these except Michael, your prince. (Dan. 10:10–21)

Here we get the notion of Michael as a prince, which is the basis for identifying him as an archangel—a prince among the angels. Two chapters later, Daniel prophesies about Michael's role at the end of time with imagery that strikingly parallels the book of Revelation:

> At that time there shall arise Michael,
> the great prince,
> guardian of your people;

> It shall be a time unsurpassed in distress
> since the nation began until that time.
> At that time your people shall escape,
> everyone who is found written in the book.
> Many of those who sleep
> in the dust of the earth shall awake;
> Some to everlasting life,
> others to reproach and everlasting disgrace.
> But those with insight shall shine brightly
> like the splendor of the firmament,
> And those who lead the many to justice
> shall be like the stars forever.
>
> As for you, Daniel, keep secret the message and seal the book until the end time; many shall wander aimlessly and evil shall increase. (Dan. 12:1–4)

We see again this role of Michael as protector of the people of God—then Israel, now the Church. He is the general of the armies of God in spiritual warfare, a constant champion for us, on whom we can call in prayer. In the New Testament, twice we read about Michael specifically in battle or disputation with the devil. In the brief letter of Jude, the second-to-last book of the Bible, the writer refers to a fight between Michael and the devil over the body of Moses.[20] The writer, in order to rebuke the pride of false teachers of the Gospel, praises the archangel's humility, since Michael does not pass judgment on the devil but refers to the judgment of the Lord:

[20] This, according to the notes in the Revised Standard Version, Catholic Edition, is apparently in reference to a piece of pious literature called the "Assumption of Moses," which was not accepted into the canon of Scripture.

> Yet the archangel Michael, when he argued with the devil in a dispute over the body of Moses, did not venture to pronounce a reviling judgment* upon him but said, "May the Lord rebuke you!" (1:9)

Lastly and perhaps most famously, Michael appears in the book of Revelation in a vision of the very beginning of time:

> Then war broke out in heaven; Michael and his angels battled against the dragon. The dragon and its angels fought back, but they did not prevail and there was no longer any place for them in heaven.
>
> The huge dragon, the ancient serpent, who is called the Devil and Satan, who deceived the whole world, was thrown down to earth, and its angels were thrown down with it. (12:7–9)

Michael, with the power of humble reliance on God, continues to fight for and with us today, and will until the very end.

In addition to his roles in angelic warfare and as guardian of the Church, Michael is also said to be a steadfast companion as death approaches, a source of strength for final perseverance in faith. Lastly, tradition teaches that he will be present at the Last Judgment to weigh the merits of souls before the Lord. Due to these extraordinary duties and patronages, St. Michael the Archangel has played a special role in the spiritual lives of Christians since the very beginning of the Church. And he has taken part in several miracles performed by God.

St. Michael in Christian History

There is a large limestone cave in Gargano, Italy, that was a site of pagan worship in Greek and Roman times. The story of how the cave was transformed into a church dedicated to St. Michael is partially told in a collection of stories called the *Liber de apparitione Sancti Michaelis in Monte Gargano*, which first appeared in the ninth century. It is also recorded in the *Acta Sanctorum* by the Bollandists, a Jesuit organization that has studied the lives of the saints since the mid-1600s. The documents are in Latin, but scholarly studies of the story are available in English.[21] Additionally, in the Middle Ages, a very popular collection of stories about many saints, called *The Golden Legend*, was written. It included the stories about Michael from Gargano as well as his appearances in other places. This book was translated into English toward the end of the thirteenth century.[22]

Sometime between the third and eight century, likely around 490, a wealthy noble named Elvio Emanuele was searching for a bull that had wandered from his herd on the slopes of the mountain. He found it stuck in the entrance to a cave. Angry at the bull for being unmanageable, he tried to have it shot with an arrow by a servant, but somehow the arrow came back and struck the archer himself. (In another version of the story, Elvio shot the arrow himself.) The noble went to Bishop Maiorano of Sipontum—who was later canonized and is now known as St. Lorenzo Maiorano—and recounted the strange events. The bishop, sensing something supernatural was afoot, ordered three

[21] John Charles Arnold, "Arcadia Becomes Jerusalem: Angelic Caverns and Shrine Conversion at Monte Gargano," *Speculum* 75, no. 3 (2000): 567–588.

[22] Jacobus de Voragine, *The Golden Legend; or, Lives of the Saints, as Englished by William Caxton* (London: J. M. Dent, 1900). A searchable scanned version of *The Golden Legend* from the Princeton library is available online: https://catalog.hathitrust.org/Record/008622445.

days of prayer and penance. At the end of the third day, St. Michael appeared to the bishop, saying:

> Know ye that this man is so hurt by my will. I am Michael the archangel, which will that this place be worshipped in earth, and will have it surely kept. And therefore I have proved that I am keeper of this place by the demonstrance and showing of this thing.[23]

After this apparition, the people and the bishop made a procession to pray at entrance of the cave. Two years later, likely in 492, the region was attacked by the pagan king Odoacer, and the Christian forces were all but defeated. Bishop Maiorano negotiated a three-day truce with the barbarians, during which the people prayed and did penance. But then St. Michael appeared to the bishop and promised help if they would attack the enemy. During the ensuing battle, a storm of sand and hail broke out that terrified the barbarians, who fled. Once more the bishop led a procession to the cave to thank St. Michael, but he did not enter, still unwilling to claim the cave for Michael since the place had been considered sacred by local pagans. Bishop Maiorano asked Pope Gelasius I for advice, and the Holy Father told him to occupy the cave and to consecrate it a church.

When they arrived to consecrate the cave, Michael appeared to the bishop again. This time, he explained that it was not necessary to consecrate the cave as it had already been consecrated by Michael's presence. The bishop entered and found an altar covered with a red cloth with a crystal cross on top. He had a church built at the front of the cave and dedicated it to St. Michael on September 29, 493.

[23] De Voragine, *The Golden Legend*, 182.

And so, at the archangel's direction, the cave was turned into a church, and it became known throughout the world in a short time. The region took the name of St. Michael, and the sanctuary became one of the four major pilgrimage sites in all of Europe for centuries. St. Francis of Assisi did not feel worthy to enter but prayed for thirty days and nights outside the cave. Later, St. Padre Pio would send people needing deliverance from evil spirits to the cave, and they were healed. The cave has been visited by pilgrims, kings, queens, popes, and saints ever since.

The cave and the sanctuary built out of it returned to prominence in the seventeenth century, when, in 1656, a plague was ravaging Naples and the surrounding countryside. The bishop, Alfonso Puccinelli, pleaded to St. Michael the Archangel for help. At dawn on September 22, after three days of fervent prayer and fasting, St. Michael appeared and promised that those who reverently kept small stones from the cave in their homes and prayed earnestly would be saved from the epidemic. And indeed the words were fulfilled. In memory of this miracle, the bishop erected a statue of St. Michael in front of his palace and added the inscription: "Prince of angels, conqueror of the plague."[24]

Stones from St. Michael's cave are still distributed today, both as general sacramentals and as relics, especially to help against the demonic. (There is a common misunderstanding that Michael promised that the stones would liberate people from demons, but this actually referred to the plague.) Michael's role in defeating Satan (Rev. 12:7–10) and his consecration of the cave makes the idea of the stones' efficacy reasonable, though,

[24] Karolina Szydłowska, "Niepokonany zwycięzca zarazy," Michalici.pl, May 3, 2020, https://michalici.pl/artykul/niepokonany-zwyciezca-zarazy.

and many exorcists around the world have used stones from the cave in their rites, with effects similar to those of relics of other saints.

St. Michael also intervened in other plagues through the ages and is for this reason considered a patron against sickness (in addition to his many other titles and works). The first known worldwide epidemic of bubonic plague took place in the sixth century AD, killing tens of millions, and it hit Rome especially hard in 590. Plagues were interpreted as a chastisement from God, and so Christians arranged processions of icons of Mary in the streets. A young deacon who would later become Pope St. Gregory the Great organized many of the processions, and at the end of one of them, he saw an apparition of St. Michael atop Hadrian's Mausoleum in Rome, and the archangel sheathed his flaming sword. This was taken to signify that the wrath of God had been appeased, and the plague stopped. The mausoleum was renamed the Castel Sant'Angelo, and today a statue of the archangel can be seen where he appeared.

Over a millennium later, in 1631, during a plague of smallpox in Tlaxcala, Mexico, Catholics commemorated that apparition of St. Michael. During the procession, the archangel appeared to a young man named Diego Lazaro de San Francisco and showed him a spring that would cure people of the plague, now known as St. Michael's Well. This spring is a Church-approved apparition site of St. Michael, and its waters continue to cure people to this day.

Mont-Saint-Michel in France

In 708, St. Michael appeared to the bishop of Avranches, France, now known as St. Aubert, in a dream. The archangel told the bishop to build a church in his honor on Mont Tombe, a rocky prominence just off the country's northwest coast. The bishop ignored the dream not once, but twice. But during the third dream, St. Michael was more forceful, and Aubert finally obeyed and started building the sanctuary, which he completed on October 16 the next year.

On the day of dedication, St. Michael appeared again to St. Aubert, showing him where to strike a rock on the island. Fresh water flowed from this rock in the middle of a saltwater bay and has supplied the island to this time. St. Michael then appeared to Aubert one more time in 714 to tell him he would join his parents in Heaven in three days—and he did.

Through the ages, Mont-Saint-Michel, as that rocky island has been called ever since, has been one of the most strikingly beautiful human habitations in the world. The church and surrounding buildings seem to have risen out of the sea; at high tide especially, the place looks as if it were from a fantasy story. It was an abbey for many centuries, then a prison after the French Revolution, and now once again houses monks and nuns. The island was twice besieged during the Hundred Years' War but was never taken; it is said that St. Michael whipped up a storm that sank English ships in 1423. Christian emperors and kings often visited the island on the feast day of October 16 to honor St. Michael and to request that he protect their Christian kingdoms.

St. Michael in Modern Exorcisms

St. Michael plays a significant role in the spiritual world, and he is identified in many roles beyond defeating Satan. It is no wonder, however, that exorcists have recourse to him to assist in exorcisms, given his role in the war in Heaven. In addition to this, St. Michael was directly associated with exorcism by Pope Leo XIII.

In 1884, Pope Leo XIII ordered that certain prayers be said after every Low Mass; these were called the "Leonine Prayers." In 1886, the Prayer to St. Michael was added to the Leonine Prayers said after every Mass by the laypeople:

> St. Michael the Archangel, defend us in battle, be our protection against the wickedness and snares of the devil. May God rebuke him, we humbly pray; and do thou, O Prince of the Heavenly host, by the power of God, cast into Hell Satan and all the evil spirits who prowl about the world seeking the ruin of souls. Amen.

The 1890–1891 edition of the *Acta Sanctae Sedis* (The Acts of the Holy See) included an exorcism that could be said only by bishops and approved priests. It was intended to curb the activity of the devil against the Church.

The 1898 edition of the Roman Ritual (the book that contains most of the rites of the Church) included "Exorcism against Satan and the Fallen Angels." This is an exorcism to drive the devil away from places and things, particularly to curb his assaults on the Church. It is sometimes called the "minor exorcism." The rubric (rule) for it says: "The following exorcism can be used by bishops, as well as by priests who have this authorization from their Ordinary."[25] This rubric has never been removed or changed, though people sometimes reproduce the minor exorcism rite and

[25] *The Roman Ritual in Latin and English with Rubrics and Plainchant Notation*, vol. 2 (Boonville, NY: Preserving Christian Publishing, 1952), 223.

remove the rubric from it. It is clear that the laity may not use this prayer.

The minor exorcism that invokes St. Michael is often used as a diagnostic test for possession. This is because the solemn exorcism rite cannot be done unless the local bishop approves it, and he should do so only after enough signs of possession (knowledge of languages the person does not know, knowledge of hidden things, reaction to holy things, and preternatural strength) are documented. The minor exorcism rite can be used with permission as a diagnostic for people, as it does not require that the signs of possession be documented first. Generally, if the person is possessed, the minor exorcism is enough to force the demon to manifest and so to reveal a genuine possession that can then be tested for proofs. In oppression cases (demonic activity that does not rise to full-blown possession) the minor exorcism is usually enough to free the person completely, and sometimes possession cases are resolved just by this prayer.

Exorcists all over the world have used stones from the cave at Gargano. St. Michael promised that stones taken from the cave would help in prayers of deliverance and exorcism. The stones are not an instant exorcism for the possessed, but they do act in a similar way to first-class relics of saints that are commonly used in exorcisms.

Even the St. Michael Prayer that the laity can say has had great effect during exorcisms I have attended. Sometimes it is said in the background by the lay assistants while the exorcism is going on. We also regularly use a blessed icon of St. Michael. The theology of blessed icons is that they are a window into the spiritual reality that they depict. We have seen the demons talk to Saint Michael in the icon many times, even when the icon is held behind the persons where they cannot see it. The demons have also confessed many times that they fear St. Michael and that he is the greatest of the angels. In one case, a demon was very worn down during the exorcism and very much wanted to leave, and it yelled, "St. Michael, please cast me out!"

5

Stigmata

The Church's view on stigmata is well defined in the book *Mystical Phenomena Compared with Their Human and Diabolical Counterfeits*.[26] Written in 1926 for the Holy See, this book brings together centuries of experience with true and false supernatural events. First and most importantly, stigmata are just one of many "accessory phenomena" that can come along with divine ecstasy. This means that stigmata are not something that happen on their own, and they are not the source or center of the experience. Stigmata, like all mystical phenomena, must arise from a divine ecstasy that is already happening. Stigmata are not the important thing but rather are indications that something more profound is already occurring.

Divine ecstasy has two aspects: internal and external. The internal aspect is that the mind becomes completely fixed on, and captivated by, an experience of God. The external aspect is that the senses seem to be suspended. The person ceases to

[26] Albert Farges and S. P. Jacques, *Mystical Phenomena Compared with Their Human and Diabolical Counterfeits* (London: Burns, Oates & Washbourne, 1926; repr., Whitefish, MT: Kessinger Publishing, 2010).

respond to his environment. This is not simply falling asleep; the person usually has his eyes open. Once the ecstasy starts, the person stops responding to sound or visual stimuli. He is usually in a frozen position staring into space. This can continue for minutes or hours.

What the internal experience of God is like cannot be easily explained. St. John of the Cross turned to poetry to try to convey his direct experiences of God because they were beyond normal description. St. Teresa of Ávila, another Carmelite saint, tried to convey her inner experience of prayer by analogy to a multilayered "interior castle" in the mind. From what has been written by them and others, we can understand that the interior experience of God is so strong and so beyond normal human understanding that it cannot be fully conveyed in words.

A number of secondary phenomena have been observed alongside divine ecstasies throughout the history of the Church. These include: stigmatization (manifesting the wounds of Jesus Christ's Crucifixion on a person's body), levitation (rising or staying suspended in the air with no support), luminous effluvia (light emanating from a person), odoriferous effluvia (pleasant smells coming from a person with no normal source), mystical abstinence (living only on the daily Eucharist for weeks, months, or years without losing weight), and powers over nature (such as the ability to control the weather or animals).

The various secondary phenomena generally do not all occur in the same individual, and the particular phenomena that do occur may change over the course of a lifetime. There is, however, a typical pattern that goes along with stigmata. In most stigmata cases, the wounds, and sometimes the whole person, spontaneously exude the strong scent of flowers. This scent usually starts on Thursday afternoon or evening and continues through the stigmatic's experience of the Passion on Friday afternoon. Most stigmatics are unable to eat anything from Thursday afternoon until Friday afternoon. One possible reason is that fasting is part of the preparation of such an intimate union with Jesus and His Passion. The wounds of stigmatics may be consistently present over the years, or they may come and go with each weekly experience of the Passion story. Regardless, they never become infected in any way, which demonstrates a kind of control over nature, since infection of an open wound would be inevitable.

The stigmata, then, are an outward sign of an internal experience of God, specifically the sacrificial Crucifixion of Jesus Christ. The wounds hurt, and hurt acutely during the Passion that the stigmatic lives through each week (and sometimes on holy days in addition to Fridays). The important thing to stigmatics, though, is their internal experience of what Christ went through and sharing that suffering with Him; the wounds themselves are secondary. In fact, most stigmatics pray that the wounds be invisible so that nobody will know about them. Almost all stigmatics try to hide their wounds with gloves or head bands, unless they are told by their spiritual director or religious superior to allow the wounds to be photographed. In some cases, this prayer is answered, and the stigmatics have what is called invisible stigmata. They still fully experience the Passion narrative, the emotions Jesus went though, and His physical pains, but there are no actual wounds.

Stigmatics are living meditations on the brutal reality of the Crucifixion. They live out the same story each week in real time. They are simultaneously present in their body and aware of where they are, and they are experiencing what Jesus went though. The extent of their experience usually changes over time. They may experience more of His sadness at losing His friends and followers one week, and another week they might experience more of

His prayers to God the Father during the Passion. The physical experience also varies: some weeks their hands are very painful and "active," meaning the wounds are open and bleeding freely, while other weeks they can barely walk due to the pain in their feet. Some develop all of the wounds—hands, feet, head, side, back, and shoulder—while others receive only some. The wounds are almost always shallow, but the pain experienced is as if the wound goes all the way through.

The stigmata represent an uncomfortable side of Christianity that we usually want to avoid. Jesus said to take up our cross and follow him (Matt. 16:24). He didn't tell us we would have an easy life; He didn't promise wealth and contentment. Jesus taught this long before His Crucifixion, as a kind of prophecy of it. His disciples were well aware of Roman crucifixions; they were regular occurrences in Jerusalem. The Romans would line the roads with the crucified after uprisings to make an example of them. He told all of us to take up a painful burden and carry it to a painful end. For some reason, Jesus chooses a few people in each generation to live out this saying almost literally.

The purpose of this is not to simply make a person suffer; it is not a cruelty. God asks certain people if they are willing to bear part of the pain of the Passion; they are not forced. Usually God tells them the purpose for which He wishes them to offer their suffering, and they meditate on this purpose when they can throughout the experience. An example might be to offer the suffering for an increase in priestly vocations in the world. Another might be for a particular priest during a particular week.

Often stigmatics move through three basic states from sunset on Thursday through Friday afternoon. During a certain period, they live the experiences of Jesus so profoundly that their bodies shudder, welts rise, and blood flows. These periods are usually followed by times of blissful union with God that comfort them. Finally there are periods when they come back to their senses and can rest for a while. There is no exact schedule to this. During the painful experience of "being there," they usually offer the suffering to God the most intently. During the consolation period, they are usually swept up into ecstatic love of God and lose all sense of suffering and of the normal world. During the rest phase, they usually pray in a more regular way and regather some physical strength.

Grace transforms suffering into a blessing. This is one of the great paradoxes of Christianity: a fuller sharing in the suffering of Christ, though more uncomfortable and even painful, gives them a special relationship with Him, brings them closer to Him, and makes them more conformed to Him. And so the stigmata, while uncomfortable to look at, and even more so to experience, are in fact a beautiful symbol of the calling to be like Christ that we all share. This is certainly not to say that we should seek out suffering or desire to hurt ourselves. That is a very distorted idea. For most Christians, it is enough to offer up our trials and difficulties and unite them with Christ's sufferings. Life provides pain and discomfort because we live in a fallen world, but we can unite those sufferings with the sufferings of Christ and allow Him to transform them into grace. The Passion story gives us a way to contextualize and transform the discomforts of life; it is a powerful reality that can help us bear our own crosses.

The apostle Paul said in his Letter to the Colossians:

> Now I rejoice in my sufferings for your sake, and in my flesh I complete what is lacking in Christ's afflictions for the sake of his body, that is, the church. (1:24)

Of course, he doesn't mean that Christ's suffering was somehow insufficient, but rather that we are accorded the great privilege to participate in some way in His sufferings, for the good of all.

Paul also wrote in his Letter to the Galatians:

> Henceforth let no man trouble me; for I bear on my body the marks of Jesus. (6:17)

We don't know if Paul was referring to scars from beatings and imprisonments, or if he experienced some marks that coincided with the Crucifixion. It is clear, though, that suffering in the flesh was part of Paul's life, and he had developed a transformative relationship with that suffering.

Finally, in his Second Letter to the Corinthians, Paul gives a description of the way Christ works through and transforms our struggles:

> Our hope for you is firm, for we know that as you share in the sufferings, you also share in the encouragement. We do not want you to be unaware, brothers, of the affliction that came to us in the province of Asia; we were utterly weighed down beyond our strength, so that we despaired even of life.
>
> Indeed, we had accepted within ourselves the sentence of death, that we might trust not in ourselves but in God who raises the dead. He rescued us from such great danger of death, and he will continue to rescue us; in him we have put our hope [that] he will also rescue us again, as you help us with prayer, so that thanks may be given by many on our behalf for the gift granted us through the prayers of many. (1:7–11)

The stigmata, then, are both a reminder of Christ's presence with us and a challenging reminder that life includes suffering with Him. If our highest aim is to be conformed to Him, should we not expect to share in some of His pain? It is critical, as we consider the stigmata, that we remember that it is first a sign of grace that arises from union with God, a reminder of the power of God to transform suffering into joy. The stigmata is not something to be sought; it is something God choses for a handful of people in each generation.

The Stigmata in History

The history of the stigmata starts with St. Francis of Assisi (1181–1226). Before him there were accounts of people who inflicted the wounds of Christ on themselves in a disordered attempt to do penance, and, in fact, the word *stigmata* previously meant marks left over from self-inflicted penances. True stigmata, however, are not, and cannot be, something we do to ourselves. Like every other participation in the divine life, the stigmata is always an unearned gift from God.

St. Francis was preparing for Michaelmas, the feast of the archangel Michael, in 1224. By this time, he had withdrawn from running the order he had founded and was entering the last phase of his life. It was September 14, the feast of the Exaltation of the Cross, and he was praying on Mount Alverna, a favorite place of peace and contemplation, with two other friars. While deep in prayer, he saw a vision of a seraphim, which is the highest and most glorious rank of angel, crucified. Thomas of Celano later described the event:

> His hands and feet seemed pierced in the midst by nails, the heads of the nails appearing in the inner part of the hands and in the upper part of the feet, and their points

> over against them. Now those marks were round in the inner side of the hands and elongated on the outer side, and certain small pieces of flesh were seen like the ends of nails bent and driven back, projecting from the rest of the flesh. So also the marks of nails were imprinted in his feet, and raised above the rest of the flesh. Moreover his right side, as it had been pierced by a lance, was overlaid with a scar, and often shed forth blood, so that his tunic and drawers were many times sprinkled with the sacred blood.[27]

This is the first account of stigmata. Francis died five years later, after dictating his spiritual wisdom for his order. But he never mentioned the stigmata or bragged about it, though many were aware of it. It is said that a few brothers of the order, Pope Alexander IV, and some other prominent people saw the marks on the saint. The earliest portrait of St. Francis does not show the stigmata since it was made before he received the wounds, but all the other portraits do. After St. Francis, the word *stigmata* became specifically associated with supernatural wounds of the Crucifixion.

There is no complete accounting of stigmata cases that have occurred through history. Most people hear only of the saints who have been said to have received it. These include Anne Catherine Emmerich, Gemma Galgani, Catherine of Siena, Mary of Jesus Crucified (Mariam Baouardy), Rita of Cascia, and Padre Pio. There is also the famous case of the Servant of God Thérèse Neumann. There also have been many purported stigmatics who

[27] Thomas of Celano, *The First Life of Saint Francis* (Marion, IN: Triangle, 2000), chap. 3, par. 94; available online at https://dmdhist.sitehost.iu.edu/francis.htm

were not saints, most of whom are unknown to the world. There is no central list of stigmata cases, and the Church generally does not make statements about the authenticity of stigmata cases.

In writing the book *Stigmata: A Medieval Phenomenon in a Modern Age*,[28] Ted Harrison sought out all published accounts of the stigmata, and as his research became known, contemporary cases were brought to his attention. He places the total number of stigmatics at just over 400 since 1224. The vast majority were women (353), though the ratio has become more balanced in the 44 cases reported since 1946. Dr. Harrison thinks this has to do with shifts in the power structures of the Church in modern times. In addition, it seems that priests started displaying the stigmata only in the last hundred years.

St. Gemma Galgani provides a rich description of her own stigmata in her autobiography:

> On June 8th [1899] after Communion, Jesus told me that that evening He would give me a very great grace. I went that same day to Confession, and I told Monsignor [Monsignor Giovanni Volpi, Gemma's confessor]. He told me to be very attentive, so that I could tell him about it afterwards.
>
> Evening came, and all of a sudden, earlier than usual, I felt an interior sorrow for my sins, far deeper than I had ever experienced before. In fact, it brought me very, very close to death. After this, all the powers of my soul became recollected. I could think of nothing but my sins, and the offense that they gave to God. My memory

[28] Ted Harrison, *Stigmata: A Medieval Phenomenon in a Modern Age* (New York: St. Martin's Press, 1994).

recalled all my past sins to mind, and made me see all the torments that Jesus had suffered in order to save me. And my will made me detest them, and promise to be willing to suffer anything in order to expiate them. My mind was flooded with thoughts; thoughts of sorrow, of love, of fear, of hope and of comfort.

Following this interior recollection, I was quickly rapt out of my senses, and I found myself before my heavenly Mother. At her right stood my guardian angel, who told me to make an act of contrition. When I had finished it my blessed Mother said to me "Daughter—In the name of Jesus, your sins are forgiven." Then she added: "Jesus my Son loves you very much, and He wishes to give you a grace. Do you know how to make yourself worthy of it?" In my misery I did not know what to answer. She continued "I will be your Mother. Will you be a true daughter?" She then spread her mantle and covered me with it.

At that moment Jesus appeared with all His wounds open, but blood no longer came out of those wounds. Rather, flames of fire issued forth from them and in an instant these flames came to touch my hands, my feet and my heart. I felt as if I would die. I fell to the floor, but my Mother supported me, keeping me covered in her mantle. I had to remain several hours in that position. Finally she kissed me on my forehead, and all vanished, and I found myself kneeling on the floor. But I still felt an intense pain in my hands, feet and heart. I arose to go to bed, and I then noticed that blood was flowing from those parts where I felt pain. I covered them as well as I could, and then with the help of my angel, I was able to go to bed. These sufferings and pains, although they afflicted

> me, filled me with perfect peace. The next morning I was able to go to Communion only with great difficulty, and I put on a pair of gloves in order to hide my hands. I could hardly stand on my feet, and I thought I would die at any minute. The sufferings continued until 3pm on Friday afternoon, the solemnity of the Sacred Heart of Jesus.[29]

Here we see an example of how the stigmata comes not as a mere physical suffering, but as part of a larger mystical experience. St. Gemma describes being filled not with horror but with a perfect peace that transcended the pain. It is an experience of extraordinary intensity, with suffering, joy, sorrow, comfort, fear, and communion, all becoming almost unbearable. In the saint's account, we also see other extraordinary graces that accompanied her experience. She was asked by Mary if she wanted to consent, was warned ahead of time to prepare for the stigmata, and was assisted and consoled by her guardian angel during it.

St. Gemma's wounds returned each Thursday night and closed on Friday afternoon, usually healing completely by Saturday, or Sunday at the latest. On Friday, she would experience a spiritual ecstasy—a kind of trance—as she shared in the Passion of Jesus. When observers examined the wounds, it was clear they went all the way through her hands, and there was never any evidence that she inflicted them herself.

Her experience of the stigmata continued until three years before she died, when, in obedience to her spiritual director, she prayed that they would cease. Even so, white marks were still

[29] *The Autobiography of St. Gemma Galgani*, trans. William Browning, C.P. (London: Catholic Way Publishing, 2013), https://www.stgemmagalgani.com/2008/11/autobiography-of-saint-gemma-galgani.html

seen on her hands and feet after her death. From 1907 to 1910, her diocese examined her life as part of her cause for sainthood, which was referred to Rome in 1920. On January 5, 1933, Pope Pius XI approved two miracles submitted as proof for her beatification. Two more miracles took place after her beatification, and she was canonized on May 2, 1940, less than four decades after her death.

Notes from a Contemporary Case of Potential Stigmata

In the course of my work, I have had the occasion to investigate some claims of miracles. One of these was a potential case of stigmata that I was able to observe over many weeks. It is very important to understand that these observations and experiences are *not revealed truth* to which you must assent. Any claimed mystical experience is private revelation at best, and human misunderstanding or deception at worst. Private revelation means that a person received some information directly from God and not through the teaching function of the Church. No one is required to believe private revelation, even from the saints. In fact, there is a great danger in putting too much faith in private revelation. This has caused cults of personality to break away from the Church and to follow a novel theology that usually becomes more distorted and apocalyptic over time, until the cult self-destructs.

Some of the information from this case is presented as an example of what seems to be a contemporary stigmatic, who has been observed by a number of priests and laypeople who witnessed the various phenomenon themselves and found them compelling. I do not claim that this is a genuine case of stigmata—only that these are the facts known so far. From here on, though, for the sake of simplicity I will refer to this as a case of stigmata, and the person as the stigmatic.

Before getting into the details of the case, readers should prepare themselves. Stigmata cases are difficult to learn about. When we look at the photographs of Thérèse Neumann with blood running out of her eyes and hands, we naturally recoil. When we read the books of Anne Catherine Emmerich (which were the basis for the movie *The Passion of the Christ*), we are presented with the horrific details that go far beyond the usual Stations of the Cross. It is easy to ignore, or to become desensitized to, the reality of the Crucifixion. We see the crucifix in every church. We gaze on it, yet we rarely fully appreciate it. If the movie *The Passion of the Christ* really disturbed you, or if you are easily upset, you may want to skip to the next chapter.

Roman crucifixion was a well-defined and systematized method for killing people in the most painful and public way possible. It was meant to be a political statement in addition to a punishment. Thousands of people were crucified, and the whole process was refined and perfected. This process was more than just being nailed on the cross; it included a systematic preparation lasting a day or more, and it continued for hours after being nailed and suspended. Everything about the crucifixion had meaning. A person cannot breathe normally when suspended by the arms, causing a feeling of suffocation. The only way to draw air into the lungs is to push up with the legs. This is exploited by nailing the feet to the cross so that pushing up becomes unbelievably painful. If the person passed out from the pain, he would be lanced or wounded in specific ways to shock him back awake—but not to kill him. Usually the condemned person was ultimately killed by breaking his legs, which took away his only way to draw breath. As an aside, Roman citizens who were condemned were not crucified; they were beheaded. Crucifixion was considered too cruel a death for Roman citizens.

Finally, please know it was a difficult decision to share this story. I do not want to cause distress, but the story is distressing. There has even been a crossover to the work I do in exorcism related to this case: the demons and Satan have railed during exorcisms that this stigmatic must be stopped, that she will create too many priestly vocations in the world through offering her suffering. In addition, the stigmatic has been told during the Passion experience that Jesus wants the story written down for you, and that Jesus wants you to know how great the sacrifice He made for you was. Further, Jesus told them that the story would bring about many conversions. To be clear, the stigmatic does not want to be known in any way. The last thing she wants is anyone knowing who she is.

The Story

The stigmatic's first experience was over fifteen years ago, on a meaningful day in the Church (I am leaving out some details). It was unexpected and shocking to her. Nothing like this had ever happened before. She was at a cathedral and a priest observed the initial manifestation, which was a hole clear through the palm of her left hand. She did not injure herself; there was no workplace accident; and the wound never got infected.

She had had a reversion to the Catholic Faith a short time before the initial stigmata. She had a near-death experience when her heart stopped for more than ten minutes while she was in the hospital: she experienced being in a shifting white space of lights with the absolute knowledge that God is real, that the Catholic Church is real, and that she was loved beyond comprehension.

As soon as she awoke, she immediately demanded that a priest be found and made her confession. She has been an ardent Catholic ever since.

She was not aware of stigmata cases, and did not understand what was happening. The wound in her hand closed and healed in a few days—which is incredibly fast. The next Thursday, her left hand began to hurt, and the skin in the centers of her palm and the back of her hand became bumpy and white. She felt a compulsion to pace after sunset on Thursday, not to eat anything, and to keep pacing until dawn. Then she experienced a number of body pains until noon on Friday, followed by intense pain in her hands and her feet. She had difficulty breathing for about two or three hours, and then it stopped.

She went to medical doctors, trying to find out what was wrong with her, and several specialists tried to diagnose and treat her condition. The folder of medical tests and reports became over an inch thick. No medical treatment seemed to affect the experience. No change in medication or therapy for potential mental illness changed a thing. Eventually she started to give up seeking answers, wore a glove, and lived with it.

Over the years, she had an interior sense of what was happening, but also a powerful urge to keep that interior reality secret. She felt self-conscious about it and felt that God did not want her to share what was happening with anyone. At the same time, she, her family, and her doctors were trying to make sense of it all. As the years progressed, the physical pain and wounds would change. Sometimes it was just one hand that would form a wound and bleed; other times it would be mostly her feet. Sometimes her head would be very painful, and small wounds would appear all around it, like a crown. More recently, her right shoulder sometimes hurts deeply and a large bruise forms over it, and a painful two-inch line appears in her side. When she recently had a body scan to check for cancerous tumors, the doctor commented that she must have been impaled in the side when she was younger because of the scar tissue from a side wound in her body. She has never had an injury to her side.

The stigmatic's experiences aren't the same each week, but they are basically consistent. There is some variation in what is emphasized, but the story is always the same. The experience starts on Thursday afternoon with a feeling of apprehension. As sunset gets closer, she experiences an urge to get to a safe and secluded place to walk back and forth. She starts to become aware of Jesus and what He is doing, that He is being marched along forcefully by a number of men. She can feel that there are chains shackled to His feet and that His shoes are gone. His hands are tied and being pulled in front of him. His feet already hurt as the road is rough and the chains are heavy and hurting His ankles. The streets are painful, with many sharp objects and foul waste of all kinds.

Then she experiences the stinging cuts of wet palms being lashed against His skin by onlookers, perhaps the same people who had just welcomed Him into the temple by placing similar palms before Him. As this happens, what look like three- or four-inch paper cuts appear on the stigmatic's arms and legs; these cause her to gasp in pain. Then a wagon that is carrying large clay jars crosses their path. The wagon stops and the driver whips Jesus across the legs with the horsewhip. This causes a scream of pain from the stigmatic and throws her to the ground. Large six- to eight-inch welts rise across both legs. These welts are so severe that, seven days later, when the story starts again, they are still visible. There is a point during this journey when Jesus is kicked in the stomach and loses the last meal He had, which is the beginning of the total loss of comfort and health He enjoyed, replaced by deprivation and the abandonment by His friends.

Walking resumes shortly thereafter; the stigmatic must pace while Jesus walks in the narrative they are experiencing. This becomes labored as the feet are increasingly swollen and in pain from the chains and the rough road. Soon they arrive at the cell under Caiaphas's house.

The stigmatic feels compelled to pace exactly ten paces, turn, and pace ten paces back. In the narrative, Jesus is barefoot and still dragging heavy chains. He is not allowed to drink any water all night, and the stigmatic becomes very thirsty, no matter how much water she drinks. Jesus is forced to pace by guards; if He stops, He is whipped with a leather strap or poked with a long thin spear of wood. Usually once during the night, for entertainment, the guard whips the strap around His neck and chokes Him to the point of passing out. The stigmatic experiences this literally and is choked until she collapses.

After a few hours, the guards become drunk and distracted, and there are brief minutes when the stigmatic is allowed to rest on the floor or against the wall. If they collapse to the floor, however, they have great difficulty getting up, because they experience their feet as so swollen and cut up that it is almost too painful to do so. Their pacing becomes more and more swaying and stumbling as the hours go on. They are aware that the purpose of all this is to exhaust and dehydrate the condemned as much as possible so that the walk to Golgotha the next day is done when utterly exhausted and dehydrated—and thus as painfully as possible. This is just the beginning of the systematic torture of crucifixion.

A few hours later, Jesus becomes aware of Mary, who is outside the house at the street level, above the underground cell. He knows that some of the apostles are with her, and that it is not safe for her. He stops and touches the wall like a gentle embrace and feels her. He is able to communicate with her, mind to mind, and He tries to comfort her and give her strength for what is to come. Mary is taken away by some of the apostles because it is becoming more dangerous for her to be there. Mary's brief presence is a great consolation to Jesus. Though He is experiencing great pain and exhaustion, the loneliness of His situation is the worst part. He has gone from being loved by many friends and followers to being alone in a dark cell and utterly rejected by His people.

The stigmatic describes that Jesus can smell the campfires of people outside the building. He can hear them talking about Him. He looks up through a large hole in the ceiling and can see the night sky. The stigmatic says that He feels comfort from this, as He is in such a confined space, but the sky represents unlimited creation.

As time goes on, He—as well as the stigmatic—gets more and more thirsty. There is a bucket in the cell that inmates use to relieve themselves, but there is no water. He finds a few precious drops of water seeping through the wall or the floor. As this forced march goes on, the stigmatic will usually vomit once or twice from the experience of Christ's dehydration and pain. She gets more and more "detached," as she puts it, feeling as if she is more there than here. She knows she is pacing in a normal room, but she also, to some extent, sees the stone walls and floor. She describes this as feeling somewhat like the out-of-body experience she had when her heart stopped for ten minutes.

Some weeks, the stigmatic is thrown forcefully to the floor once or twice during the night. This is always toward a soft piece of furniture, so there is no danger of being hurt. When observed, her body seems to be genuinely, roughly, randomly *thrown*; there is no obvious force that she is applying to toss herself across the room, nor does it seem controlled by her in any way.

During one of the moments, when He is allowed to rest on the floor, Jesus prays out loud to the Father to forgive the men who are tormenting Him. The stigmatic hears Jesus praying for them in Aramaic but has an internal understanding of what the words mean. (The stigmatic knows only English.) There are weeks where the stigmatic speaks in what sounds like Aramaic at this point in the narrative, but when questioned later, she does not recall doing so.

There are breaks when the stigmatic is told to lie down and rest, and sometimes there is even a brief sleep of up to an hour. These are outside of the Passion narrative and seem to come when her body is ready to collapse from pacing too long. She will be exhausted and stumbling and mumbling, "All right, all right, I'm walking," as if talking to the guards she hears yelling at her.

Toward morning, Jesus sees Satan in the cell with Him, tempting Him to not go through with His sacrifice. One week, the stigmatic screamed at Satan—"Get out of my way!"—in a surprisingly powerful voice and then resumed pacing. Another week, she said at this point, "They are just waiting to see if I go through with it" and explained that many demons were watching Jesus.

By morning, the shift of guards has changed, and Jesus is brought out of the cell. There is a period of about forty-five minutes during which He is just waiting, sitting on the ground outside the building. The stigmatic sits and waits also. There are the remnants of campfires all over; the smell of old embers pervades the air. Jesus is mostly alone and waits in silence. He is no longer distracted by people talking to, or otherwise interacting with, Him. He is with His thoughts and His prayers to the

Father. He is still barefoot, and His feet are very swollen. His body is tired and sore. There are far fewer people about; it seems they may have gone to Pilate's in anticipation of the judgment or the beginning of the Crucifixion. Spiritually, the stigmatic can see a cloud of angels over Jesus, giving Him strength and comfort for what He must do.

Jesus is then walked to the building where Pontius Pilate lives and works and is brought into an area of the building where Jews normally are not allowed, where a non-Roman citizen could be killed for entering. Pontius Pilate is irritated at having been awakened so early, and it takes time for them to get him to appear. Jesus catches the eye of Pilate's wife, and they look at each other for a moment.

Jesus is not yet in the open area where the judgment will be passed, so He can't be sure how many people are there; but He hears angry voices, and this hurts Him greatly as they are His people. Then, while He is waiting, Jesus is beaten by someone, and He collapses. He starts to experience worry, fear, and loneliness as the judgment draws closer. The apostles are mostly off hiding and protecting His mother, Mary. Mary Magdalene is coming to the judgment, though, with at least one of the apostles. One of Lazarus's sisters, another Mary, is joining them. Pilate, finally ready, is annoyed at being bothered with this, and the Jews irritate him. He just wants to get it over with, and he sends Jesus off to be crucified. Barabbas was chosen by the people to be freed; the people chose unrepentant evil over complete good; it had to be that way.

The stigmatic next experiences the first of the even more excruciating pain and wounds: the scourging. She feels compelled to go to a banister or another part of the house where she can hold on to something. She abruptly screams and recoils from blows; after about ten minutes she is driven to her knees with her hands still holding on. Her body shakes and quivers as she experiences the torture Jesus endured. This experience goes on for some time, with deep sobbing in pain between screams. Jesus is especially upset, though, because the ground is covered with the dried blood of many previous scourgings. The Romans seem to enjoy the torture and are very professional in their work. Finally, they release His hands, and she is thrown to the floor. Some weeks, very ugly bruises and cuts appear across her back as the blows are delivered. The scourging covered everywhere on His body. His face and His lip are broken open. He could taste the metal from the implements. Usually from this point forward, the stigmatic's left eye is held closed, as it was injured in the scourging; she cannot see out of it until the Passion story ends. She describes that it feels swollen shut, and that too much blood has run into it. A Marine veteran friend of the stigmatic witnessed these scourging wounds appear once and said they were worse than those of torture victims in war.

After the scourging, the scent of flowers emanating from wounds usually becomes very pronounced. It seems to be strongest around the head but clearly also comes from the hands and feet. This scent fills the house; when a priest friend came to say Mass one Friday, he noted that the whole house smelled like a florist shop. Interestingly, the stigmatic cannot smell this aroma at all; she was surprised when other people commented on it and was initially very embarrassed.

There is then another short period of waiting. During this, the stigmatic says the Romans are searching for the largest crossbeam to make Him drag, while they laugh. The stigmatic experiences that the Romans left the vertical poles in place and made the condemned drag to the cross only a crossbeam that matched his armspan. The stigmatic then starts pacing again, this time using as much space as possible, not just ten paces at a time. This walking goes on for about forty minutes, with two collapses. She sees Simon of Cyrene help Jesus by carrying the crossbeam for a time. The stigmatic says that Simon was very scared that the Romans would accidentally crucify him, as they were already drinking. The stigmatic has not yet experienced Veronica during these episodes, but she hopes to someday. As this painful walking goes on, the stigmatic says many times, "We're almost there." One week, she also said, "We're almost there.... I'm ready."

Once they arrive at Golgotha, the stigmatic sits for about fifteen minutes. She says that she can hear other men being nailed and their screams. At this point, the stigmatic lies on the floor. Her right hand is pulled out to the side, and she lets out a long, heartbreaking scream of pain. Her body contorts with it, but her right hand seems fixed in space. As she gasps, her left hand goes out and there is another guttural scream of pain. Now she experiences the guards' showing Jesus the spike they will use on His feet. She says it is the biggest nail she has ever seen, and that she cannot believe that it can be driven through her feet. Then the worst scream of pain comes as one foot is held on top of the other. After the nailing, the stigmatic's hands become very cold to the touch, and her fingers turn pale white.

Then, when things already seem so unbelievably cruel, they get worse. The stigmatic is croaking and gasping for air. She starts to move her legs as if she is pushing up in order to breathe. She mutters, "I can't breathe, I can't breathe ..." After about fifteen minutes of this, she tries to lift her head and look at the people Jesus sees. She explains that the crown of thorns is placed such that it forces her head down. If she lifts her head, it forces the thorns deeper into the soft skin at the back of her neck. Keeping the head forward makes the neck cramp terribly after a while. Jesus wants to see His Mother and forces His head up to look with His one good eye. He sees her, and He sees the pain in her face. Jesus then sees that Mary is also upset by the many scavenger birds feeding on the dead bodies on the hill. Since it has no impact on His sacrifice, He tells the vultures to stop, and they obey Him as their Creator. He allows them to stay in the area, however, because they are doing what they were created to do. This is done solely to relieve some of the pain His mother feels.

Jesus struggles to breathe for some time, doing little more. After a while He forces His head up again and looks. He sees Thaddeus and Barnabas toward the back of the crowd looking at Him. The stigmatic says that Barnabas has a sword, and they look as if they want to take action, but they cannot. There are too many guards. Jesus feels so alone on the Cross. He feels the loss of his friends, seeing how many have abandoned Him. This is the worst part of His pain.

There are a number of difficult details about the suffering of Jesus at this point. The stigmatic describes how the rough wood of the Cross puts large splinters into His back when He pushes up with His legs to breathe. She describes the biting insects that sting His flesh, which is torn so severely in places that the insects enter one wound and exit through another. As more blood is lost, Jesus experiences seizures as His brain is starved for oxygen. The stigmatic seizes, and later describes that it felt as if her hands would be torn from the nails by the writhing. After this, Christ's vision starts to go dark. The stigmatic says that His feet and legs are numb now, but this is a relief because he can no longer feel the large spike through His feet. But, also, He cannot push up with His legs anymore. He starts to breathe by contracting His stomach muscles, but it does not work well. The stigmatic gasps that she cannot get enough air. If Jesus passes out, the guards viciously poke a sharp stick between specific lower ribs to cause maximum pain—but not threaten life. They want Him awake and experiencing as much pain as possible.

The end is coming soon now. The stigmatic says that she hears Jesus pray to the Father in Aramaic, but she does not want to speak the words, as they are in the Gospel and she is not a priest. Jesus also mutters many times, "I'm so cold, I'm so cold."

She feels Christ's loneliness even more toward the end. Jesus is devastated that His friends have left him. He looks one last time and sees His mother and John the beloved. In addition, Jesus sees an endless sea of the souls of the people He is about to save, all of those who had lived before and would live after this moment. The stigmatic says that it is an indescribable number, billions. In the last moments, she feels His body panic as He cannot breathe, and she feels His fear. She then stops breathing for a minute or so. Internally she feels Him die, and suddenly He just isn't there anymore. She has a feeling during this that she is so with Him and so little in the "real world" that she will be taken with Him when He dies—that she will die also. Then she wakes up completely herself, back to normal.

This is the basic experience the stigmatic has endured every week for the last fifteen years, plus some additional holy days. Outside of these two days a week, she has lived a normal life of raising children, taking care of parents, and just living life.

There was an interesting coda that occurred after one week's passion experience. The stigmatic has no training in ancient languages, or any language at all besides English. During the Passion, I heard her saying some words that sounded like Aramaic, something like "aboon deshemiah." I did not know what they meant, but I wondered if it might be the Our Father. After everything was over. I played a recording of the prayer for the stigmatic. She was immediately able to sing the prayer along with the recording, but then she frowned and stopped. She said there was something off about it, something wrong. I looked more closely and discovered that I had played a recording of the prayer in *Syrian* Aramaic, which is slightly different from *Jewish* Aramaic. I found a Jewish Aramaic recording, and she was able to sing along with all the words.

I then looked up the prayer written out in Jewish Aramaic and showed it to the stigmatic. The first words were "Abwoon d'bwashmaya Nethqadash shmakh." I struggled to say them and failed. But when she looked at them, she immediately pronounced them fluently. I checked her pronunciation against the recording again, and it was correct. The stigmatic had heard Jesus say this prayer in the Passion vision so many times that it had become part of her.

The stigmatic has felt recently that Jesus wants to convey through her the importance of the Our Father—that it is a kind of participation in His sacrifice, a submission to the will of the Father. The stigmatic experienced Jesus' sharing that most people do not say the Our Father with enough heart and intent; it is not meant to be said as a casual and thoughtless prayer. It is also not a simple prayer. Aramaic, like Hebrew, is a very complex language. Each word has a number of meanings, from its concrete and straightforward meaning to its abstract and spiritual meanings. The Our Father can be translated a number of ways; there is not just one rendering of each word that is valid. In addition, the prayer was translated to Greek, then into Latin, and finally into English. There are translation decisions and compromises that must be made at each level.

A proof of this difficulty is the fact that on June 7, 2019, the Apostolic See changed the Italian translation from "lead us not into temptation" to "do not abandon us to temptation," in the prayers of the Mass. This change removes any misunderstanding that God could actively move us to sin. The Church has the deep expertise to wrestle with the nuances of translating the Our Father and other aspects of the Tradition. It is our job to deepen our personal relationship with God through its heartfelt use. The two messages the stigmatic experienced that Jesus wants to convey are that (1) the sacrifice for our souls was far deeper than most of us appreciate and (2) that we need to appreciate the depth and power of the Lord's Prayer.

Our Father who art in heaven,
hallowed be Thy name;
Thy kingdom come.
Thy will be done
on earth, as it is in heaven.
Give us this day our daily bread,
and forgive us our trespasses,
as we forgive those who trespass against us;
and lead us not into temptation,
but deliver us from evil.
Amen.

Jesus loves you so, so much.

6

The Incorruptibles

In 1977, Joan Carroll Cruz wrote a thoroughly researched book on the incorruptible saints called *The Incorruptibles*.[30] Before this, there had been no thorough treatment of the topic, though some general phenomena were described by Fr. Herbert Thurston in his 1952 book, *The Physical Phenomena of Mysticism*.[31] There were also many simple references to incorruptibility in the *Acta Sanctorum*, the official account of the saints published by the Jesuits.

Cruz described her motivations for writing the book—to dispel false impressions and get at the truth of incorruptibility—in its preface:

> In a number of European churches there can be found crystal reliquaries that contain reclining statues representing particular Saints, the bones of the Saints being enclosed in their stimulated figures. Because of the

[30] Joan Carroll Cruz, *The Incorruptibles: A Study of the Incorruption of the Bodies of Various Catholic Saints and Beati* (Rockford, IL: TAN Books, 1977).

[31] Herbert Thurston, S.J., *The Physical Phenomena of Mysticism* (Guildford, UK: White Crow Books, 2013); originally published in 1952 by Henry Regnery, Chicago.

> techniques employed in reproducing pictures of some of these models, the figures have been frequently mistaken for the actual bodies, producing errors such as that involving St. Francis of Geronimo ... and creating false rumors, as occurred with regard to St. Frances Cabrini, whose body was never found preserved.

Cruz worked with various shrines that host seemingly incorrupt bodies and found that, in many cases, the remains had been damaged or destroyed by fires, floods, or persecutors of the Church. It also turned out that, in many cases, the relics were not in the shrine, the city, or even the country where they were purported to be. Record keeping was usually subpar, and so inaccuracies about the number and perfection of incorruptibles had seeped into the Catholic consciousness.

This is not to say, however, that the entire concept has been disproved—far from it! Rather, it is a reminder that the Church continues to appeal to the very best science in the claims she makes about miracles, including correcting impressions that had been based on mistaken or out-of-date information. In many cases, Cruz does an excellent job of relating the story of past incorruptible saints that their orders provided to her. There are a number of incorruptible saints whose remains are still available or were so well known over history that there is no doubt of their validity.

It is important to begin this topic with an overview of how the body changes after death in normal circumstances. Without any intervention, human or divine, the corpse normally decomposes like any other organic matter. Depending on the climate and the soil, an unembalmed body buried without a coffin takes eight to twelve years to decompose to a skeleton. In extraordinary cases, though, natural circumstances such as extreme dryness and cold can cause the process to be delayed indefinitely. One example is the famous "Iceman" found in 1991 in the Alps; he had been largely preserved by the ice for about five thousand years.

Humans can also step in to arrest the normal process. The preservation afforded by embalming varies based on a number of factors: how quickly the body was embalmed after death, the thoroughness of the embalming, the type and quality of the casket, the airtightness of the vault, and so on. In some cases, an embalmed body may be perfectly preserved twenty years later, while in others, it may begin to decompose within a year or two. In the rare cases in which bodies are regularly maintained, the preservation can last much longer. The body of Vladimir Lenin is still on display in Moscow in a good state of preservation after ninety-five years. Famously, the ancient Egyptians developed embalming techniques that, when combined with the dry climate, have led to some preservation for three thousand years or more. It is important to note that embalming techniques were therefore known in the ancient world for about three thousand years before Christ.

In all of these cases, though, bodies found preserved by intentional or accidental means are stiff, discolored, and partially skeletal. This is in stark contrast to the bodies of saints deemed incorrupt by the Church. In many of the recognized cases, for instance, the bodies were in no position to be preserved by natural circumstance—and sometimes were even exposed to water, which normally speeds up decomposition—and were never embalmed at all. In spite of this, they are often found lifelike and flexible, sometimes even with a sweet aroma. In addition, examiners often observe a clear serum exuded from the body over time.

One may reasonably wonder why God would demonstrate His power in this way. It may be a miraculous sign that serves to confirm something from a holy person's life. For instance, St. Bernadette Soubirous received the message, "I am the Immaculate Conception," from Mary, which confirmed the recently defined dogma of the Church. Bernadette's incorruptibility may be, at least in part, a confirmation from Heaven of the validity of her visions and of this dogma of the Church.

The incorrupt saints also serve as a sign of comfort and hope to many people. Their pure bodies point to the immortality of the soul, a confirmation that these persons were and remain special in a supernatural way. Though they may not still be alive on earth, and their souls are no longer there, their bodies become a sign of godliness. Thus, incorruptibility is a reminder of the intrinsic connection between the body and the soul. A person is defined as the union of a soul and a body. If the souls of incorrupt persons have attained Heaven, then their bodies may also show some supernatural traits.

St. Cecilia (d. 177)

St. Cecilia was the first saint found to be incorrupt. She came from a wealthy Roman family but converted to Christianity at a young age and took a vow of virginity. Nevertheless, her family married her to a nobleman named Valerian, but she convinced him to honor her vow. Valerian later converted to Christianity after seeing a vision of his wife's guardian angel.

Cecilia helped to bury Christians who had been martyred by the Roman authorities along the main road in the city, the Appian Way. This act was considered a crime against the empire. They tried to kill her by confining her to the steam bath in her home for an entire day and night, but she survived. Then they sent a professional executioner to behead her, but after the three blows allowed by Roman law, she again survived, though she was critically wounded. Cecilia remained on the floor praying for three days and nights, and when she finally died, she was found with four fingers extended: three on one hand, one on the other—a reference to the Blessed Trinity and the one true God.

Her fellow Christians placed her body, in the same position in which it had been found, in a casket with her clothing and the fabric used to recover her blood. The future Pope Urban recorded where she was buried. Several centuries later, in 822, Pope Paschal I went to move her remains to a newly renovated cathedral. Workers could not find her remains where they were supposed to be, but the Holy Father received a vision telling him where they were. Her body was found there, intact and preserved, along with the bones of her husband and his brother. They were all moved to the new location.

During another restoration of the cathedral, in 1599, two white sarcophagi were uncovered near the high altar. Cardinal Paolo Emilio Sfondrati had them opened in the presence of witnesses, who observed her body to be still intact in the same position. Her fingers were in the same position described at her death nearly fourteen centuries previously. The bloody clothes were present and the wound in her neck was clearly visible. It had been over seven hundred years since she had been buried a second time without embalming. Cardinal Sfondrati took a small bit of cloth with her blood on it and gave tiny pieces to a number of other cardinals. He later discovered a chip of her bone on the fabric, which he treasured as a relic. The cathedral displayed her body for a short time for the faithful to venerate;

then, after a high Mass, it was reinterred under the high altar of the cathedral dedicated to her.

While we don't have modern scientific analysis of St. Cecilia's incorruptibility, we do have something close to an experiment. Her husband and brother-in-law died about the same time and were likely treated in the same way after they died. Their bodies were not exposed to any conditions different from what Cecilia's body had been exposed to, yet they had decayed to skeletons by the ninth century, as one would expect. Further, the fact that Cecilia was found with blood on her clothes indicates that her body was not cleaned or treated in any way before burial.

St. Cecilia's incorrupt body points to the virtues she displayed in life, which were those displayed by many of the martyrs of the early Roman Church: chastity, fortitude, and an abiding faith in the goodness of the Lord. She placed her faith and her commitment to God before the world, and the world rejected her for it. She refused to renounce God. The final sign carried forward by her incorrupt body is the silent affirmation of the truth and perfection of the dogma of the Trinity.

St. Catherine of Siena (1347–1380)

St. Catherine of Siena's life was full of miracles. She could be featured in almost any chapter of this book. While the preservation of her remains isn't as striking as that of some other saints, her story illustrates in a particular way the increasing interest in relics that we saw in St. Cecilia's story.

St. Catherine was a pious child who, like Cecilia, made a vow of virginity early in life. She started having religious visions as a child, and they seem to have led to a maturity beyond her years. She practiced mortification of the body from an early age, fasting and wearing a hair shirt to remind her that her final comfort would be in Heaven, not here on Earth. She was determined to enter the Order of St. Dominic, which was at that time primarily a penitential order. Over her mother's objections she became a lay member at the age of seventeen and spent her first three years in the order in isolation at home, praying and doing penance.

At the age of twenty, she expanded her efforts to the corporal works of mercy: caring for the sick, ministering to the imprisoned, and distributing alms to the poor. She was also known to free many from demonic possession, to perform miracles of healing, and to levitate during times of prayer. For one period of her life, she subsisted on the Eucharist alone, not needing regular food at all. She bore the stigmata, though she prayed that the marks would not be visible to other people. After her death, the marks became visible to all. When plague struck in the 1370s, she fearlessly cared for the sick, prepared people for death, and buried them herself.

Concerned over the Papal Schism of 1378, she offered her life to God for the graces for the Church to heal. She died in Rome on April 29, 1380, while on a mission of diplomacy and grace in defense of the true pope. She was not buried until 1385, when her casket was placed aboveground near the Rosary Chapel of the Church of Santa Maria sopra Minerva. During the transition, her head was removed and sent to Siena, where she had lived and performed her miracles and where it can be seen to this day. It is mummified, but all the skin is intact over six centuries years later.

St. Teresa of Ávila (1515–1582)

St. Teresa of Ávila was born into a noble family in Spain and, like Catherine of Siena, was very pious even as a child. At the age of seven, she wanted to travel to convert the Moors—Muslims living in Spain and other nearby areas—and to die a martyr. She later joined the Carmelites in Ávila in 1534 at the age of nineteen. The order had relaxed its rule, and socializing was common. Two decades into her time in the monastery, Teresa read *The Confessions of Saint Augustine* and experienced a profound conversion. Against great opposition, she undertook a reform of the order that restored its traditions of prayer and contemplation. It was then, when she started living under the restored rule, that she began to experience visions, levitations, and harassing visits from the devil.

Teresa died in 1582 at the age of sixty-seven, and was buried the day after her death—but with an odd complication. The main donor supporting the convent demanded that heaps of rubble and large stones be piled on top of the coffin to ensure that nobody could take the body away. But the coffin could not support the weight, and it collapsed. The sweet fragrance that people had smelled around Teresa during life, and immediately after her death, emanated from the grave site. Only nine months later, the nuns got permission to satisfy their curiosity about the fragrance by exhuming the body and examining it.

The coffin was rotting from the moisture and earth that had intruded when it collapsed, and the saint's clothes were ruined and rotted by mildew and mold. Teresa's body, however, was found intact and unharmed, looking "as fresh and whole as if it had only been buried the day before." The nuns cleaned her body and dressed her in a fresh habit. The provincial decided to take her right hand as a relic, noting that the hand exuded an oil, and he had it placed in a reliquary in Ávila.

After some disputes about who would retain the body, it was entrusted to the monastery in Ávila. Bishop Pedro Fernández de Temiño brought two medical doctors to examine the body.

> The doctors examined the body and decided that it was impossible that its condition could have a natural explanation, but that it was truly miraculous . . . for after three years, without having been opened or embalmed, it was in such a perfect state of preservation that nothing was wanting to it in any way, and a wonderful odor issued from it.[32]

Over time, experts examined the body on several occasions, and more relics were taken. In 1872, the heart was examined, since Teresa had written that an angel had repeatedly pierced her heart with a lance. First, it is amazing that her heart even could be examined in 1872, as it had been 290 years since her death. But more than that, two doctors found a perforation in her heart that they could not explain. A final examination of the body took place in 1914, and again she was found to be in the same condition as in previous examinations—and the same pleasant fragrance still emanated from her.

St. John of the Cross (1542–1591)

St. John of the Cross was a contemporary of Teresa of Ávila. In 1563, at the age of twenty-one, he joined the Carmelite Order, and he was ordained a priest five years later. He was drawn specifically to the stricter religious life of the original order and collaborated with Teresa to reform the Carmelites. The resistance was so intense that he was kidnapped and imprisoned for nine months, but eventually he and Teresa achieved positions of influence in the order.

[32] Cruz, *The Incorruptibles*, 164.

St. John's classic works of mysticism include *The Ascent of Mount Carmel*, *The Dark Night of the Soul*,[33] and *The Spiritual Canticle*.[34] These can be placed alongside the writings of Teresa of Ávila, such as *The Way of Perfection*[35] and *The Interior Castle*,[36] to form the primary expression of mystical spirituality in the Catholic Church.

John of the Cross died in 1591, at the age of forty-nine, in Úbeda, Spain. At his funeral, the faithful crowded to touch objects to his body, which they trusted had been sanctified by his life. They were right: a few days after the burial beneath the church, the friars saw a bright light shining over where he lay. Then, eighteen months after his death, Church authorities ordered that his bones be removed to a location prepared for them in Segovia, Spain. When they opened the tomb, there was a fragrant odor, and they saw that the body had not decomposed at all. The Carmelite prior then refused the order, since it stipulated that John's *bones* be transferred and there was instead an intact body. To demonstrate the lack of deterioration, a finger was cut off—and the wound bled.

Nine months later, they returned to finish the job, whether the prior liked it or not, and found the body still intact. They put

[33] *The Complete Words of St. John of the Cross, Doctor of the Church*, vol. 1, *General Introduction, Ascent of Mount Carmel, Dark Night of the Soul* (Whitefish, MT: Kessinger Publishing, 2010). Also available online.

[34] *The Complete Words of St. John of the Cross, Doctor of the Church*, vol. 2, *Spiritual Canticle, Poems* (Whitefish, MT: Kessinger Publishing, 2010). Also available online.

[35] St. Teresa of Ávila, *The Way of Perfection* (Mineola, NY: Dover Publications, 2012). Also available online.

[36] St. Teresa of Ávila, *Interior Castle* (Mineola, NY: Dover Publications, 2007). Also available online.

it in a bag and left, and the pleasant odor that emanated from the body caused many to inquire about what was in the bag. After arriving in Segovia, the body was put on display for the people and then entombed. Further examinations of the body occurred in 1859 and 1909, with no changes in its condition observed. The last examination was in 1955, at which time the body was slightly discolored but still flexible and moist 364 years after his death.

St. Charbel Makhlouf (1828–1898)

St. Charbel is perhaps the most remarkable case of incorruption we have, given that he lived and died relatively recently, and that the preservation is so extensive. St. Charbel was born in 1828 in northern Lebanon. He came from a poor but very religious family and was drawn to solitude and prayer from his earliest years. When he was twenty-three, he entered the Monastery of St. Maroun Annaya, and he was ordained a priest when he was thirty years old. He spent sixteen years in the regular monastery and then was given permission to move to its hermitage.

For twenty-three years, St. Charbel lived the hermit life thoroughly: he slept on the ground, ate sparingly once per day, wore a hair shirt, practiced corporal discipline, and spent almost all his time in prayer. At the age of seventy, he suffered a seizure as he was celebrating Mass. He died eight days later on Christmas Eve 1898. The custom of his monastery (which is fairly common) was to bury monks in the earth without embalming or coffins.

For forty-five nights after he was buried, his fellow monks observed a bright light above his grave. The lights continued off and on, and a few months later, the monastery requested permission to exhume his body. There had recently been torrential rains, so when they turned up the earth, they found his body floating in water and mud—normally the kind of conditions that would hasten decomposition. Charbel's remains, however, were in perfect condition. They cleaned him and clothed him in a fresh habit, placing his body in a casket in the chapel. Charbel's body exuded a substance they described as a mixture of blood and perspiration; it moistened his garments such that they had to reclothe his body twice a week.

In 1927, twenty-nine years after his death, two medical doctors examined his body. They sealed all the documentation related to the examination in a fresh coffin with the body, then sealed the coffin with zinc and walled it up in a dry cavity in the chapel. The coffin remained there for twenty-three years, until 1950.

In 1950, pilgrims visiting the chapel noticed a fluid seeping out of the wall where St. Charbel was entombed. The monastery was concerned that there may have been damage to the body, so they obtained permission to break the seal on the coffin and examine it. Witnesses from the Vatican, the religious order, and the medical profession observed the process. His body was found free of decay, flexible, and lifelike. The moisture that was seeping out of his tomb had come from his body, which continued to exude the same fluid that had been observed decades previously. The fabric that was pressed against his body to absorb the fluid has been said to have effected many cures by being touched to ailing people. The miracles for his beatification seemed to have been connected to his incorrupt body in some way.

The first miracle chosen for his beatification was the healing of Maria Abel Kamari, a thirty-three-year-old nun. In 1936, she became ill and developed gastric ulcers that stopped her from eating much. They did multiple surgeries but could not fix the problem. She developed secondary problems, including osteoporosis. By 1942, she was bedridden. On July 11, 1950, she asked to be taken to Charbel's tomb. When she touched the tomb, she felt a shock go through her body. She took a bit of the oil that seeped from his tomb and touched the sick parts of her body with it. She immediately rose and was able to walk normally.

The second miracle for his beatification was the healing of Iskander Obeid. He was a blacksmith who damaged his right eye severely in 1925 and again in 1937. He refused to let the doctors remove the eye, which no longer worked. In 1950, he started praying to Charbel for a cure. Iskander had a dream in which Charbel told him to visit his tomb. He did and he spent a long time praying there. That night, he had another dream in which Charbel blessed him. He woke being able to see with his right eye and having no pain for the first time since 1925.

In 1965, the postulator for Charbel's cause for canonization certified that his body remained intact with no alteration from its previous state. Pilgrims continued to flock to his monastery, and three miracles were attributed to his intercession, including a woman with serious deformities who stood upright for the first time in her life while praying at his tomb.

Then, in 1976, after Charbel's beatification, his body was found completely decomposed; only bones remained. We might surmise that once the miracles that confirmed his sainthood had been observed and confirmed, God allowed the body to revert to its natural condition.

Incorruptibility and Relics

Incorruptibility is not a precisely defined phenomenon. Sometimes it is dramatically beyond what should be possible, as in the case of St. Cecilia, and sometimes it is less dramatic, such as the head of St. Catherine of Siena. Incorruptibility does not mean the body is perfect, but rather that it is more preserved and lifelike than it should be. It is important to note that for the purpose of approving sainthood and devotions, the Church does not put much stock in whether a person's body seems to be incorrupt. While incorruptibility used to be considered a miracle that implied sainthood, it is now considered only a favorable sign. What validates saints are their lives and objectively verified miracles connected with them, not the states of their bodies. Not all saints are or were incorrupt; in fact, only a tiny portion of them have been.

In looking at the history of incorrupt bodies, we see part of the development of the tradition of venerating first-class relics. A first-class relic is a piece of the body of a saint (or anything from the Passion of Jesus); a second-class relic is something that a saint owned in life; and a third-class relic is something that has been touched to a first-class relic. The practice of taking and using relics was one of the main issues that led to the Protestant Reformation. The Council of Trent was called in response to the challenges of the Protestant Reformation in 1545. In the section on the veneration of relics and saints, the council says:

> The holy Synod enjoins on all bishops, and others who sustain the office and charge of teaching, that, agreeably to the usage of the Catholic and Apostolic Church, received from the primitive times of the Christian religion, and agreeably to the consent of the holy Fathers, and to the decrees of sacred Councils, they especially instruct the faithful diligently concerning the intercession and invocation of saints; the honour (paid) to relics; and the legitimate use of images: teaching them, that the saints, who reign together with Christ, offer up their own prayers

to God for men; that it is good and useful suppliantly to invoke them, and to have recourse to their prayers, aid, (and) help for obtaining benefits from God, through His Son, Jesus Christ our Lord, who is our alone Redeemer and Saviour; but that they think impiously, who deny that the saints, who enjoy eternal happiness in heaven, are to be invocated; or who assert either that they do not pray for men; or, that the invocation of them to pray for each of us even in particular, is idolatry; or, that it is repugnant to the word of God; and is opposed to the honour of the one mediator of God and men, Christ Jesus; or, that it is foolish to supplicate, vocally, or mentally, those who reign in heaven. Also, that the holy bodies of holy martyrs, and of others now living with Christ,—which bodies were the living members of Christ, and the temple of the Holy Ghost, and which are by Him to be raised unto eternal life, and to be glorified,—are to be venerated by the faithful; through which (bodies) many benefits are bestowed by God on men; so that they who affirm that veneration and honour are not due to the relics of saints; or, that these, and other sacred monuments, are uselessly honoured by the faithful; and that the places dedicated to the memories of the saints are in vain visited with the view of obtaining their aid; are wholly to be condemned, as the Church has already long since condemned, and now also condemns them.

Miracles happen in the lives of saints. Is it not unreasonable to expect them to happen after they die? In the Christian view, the person is two parts: a soul and a body joined. That whole person is separated at death, with the soul (for the saint) residing in Heaven and the body remaining here. The two will be reunited in a new way with a glorified body when Jesus returns. The body left here now is still the saint's body, however. It is still part of the entire person. This is perhaps why God allows miracles associated with relics, and why we see demons identifying the saints' relics that are applied to them, showing great fear of the saints' power. And it is also perhaps why the holiness of a person's soul is manifested in his or her body after death, through the miracle of incorruptibility.

7

Levitation

Pierre-Simon Laplace, the great French mathematician who helped develop the scientific method, famously said, "The weight of evidence for an extraordinary claim must be proportional to its strangeness." This was simplified by Carl Sagan into, "Extraordinary claims require extraordinary evidence." Levitation is an extraordinary claim, to be sure. It is also a claim that is very concrete: it is something anyone can observe readily if it occurs. But unlike incorruption, its effects are not lasting, so we have to rely on eyewitness accounts.

As with all claims of the miraculous, the Church has been doubtful and on guard against exaggeration or fabrication. There is a tendency for second- and third-hand stories to evolve over time into greater myths. Having direct testimony from the person who levitated, or from those who witnessed the person levitating, is very important—and even then, the Church keenly examines the reliability and motivations of witnesses. An example of this kind of investigation can be found in claims about St. Francis of Assisi.

St. Bonaventure was born in 1221, five years before Francis died. He entered the Order of Friars Minor (the Franciscans) and became the order's seventh leader. While mostly known as a philosopher, Bonaventure also wrote about his order's founder, including the claim that St. Francis was often found floating in the air during spiritual ecstasies. Reports from later writers echoed and expanded on these claims, saying that St. Francis would soar to the treetops and sometimes into the sky, where he could barely be seen.

The difficulty is that in 1245 (nineteen years after he had died), a detailed investigation into Francis's life had been made by the Church. Authorities interviewed many people who knew him, and none of them mentioned levitation. In checking all the other documents that survived to the modern era, Herbert Thurston, S.J., also found no mention of levitation related to St. Francis.[37] So, either St. Bonaventure had access to materials that have not survived, or the stories of levitation were an invention that Bonaventure heard and repeated as fact. We are often led to believe that people before the modern era, especially in the Church, were easily duped or indifferent to facts, but the Church has, throughout her history, applied the best methods available to her to get at the truth of miracles.

A similar pattern happened with St. Dominic. None of his followers who knew him and documented his virtues and prayer life ever mentioned his levitating, and no early biographers mention it either. Yet, fifty or sixty years after his death, reports of his levitating started to appear in accounts of his life. This same thing happened in accounts of the lives of St. Ignatius of Loyola and St. Francis Xavier. Rarely were the development of these claims due to deception: rather, pious writers passed on stories that emerged from those devoted to the saints. Given this pattern,

[37] Herbert Thurston, S.J., *The Physical Phenomena of Mysticism* (1952; Guildford, UK: White Crow Books, 2013), 5–7.

should we dismiss all claims of levitation in the lives of the saints? No, it seems not.

There is good reason to believe, for instance, that St. Teresa of Ávila levitated on a number of occasions. Her levitations were witnessed repeatedly by many people. We also have the saint's own accounts: she described the experience in her autobiography. Although she preferred not to discuss such matters, she wrote the book under obedience to her superior. Here she describes how she resisted these raptures that sometimes led to levitation:

> These effects are very striking. One of them is the manifestation of the Lord's mighty power: as we are unable to resist His Majesty's will, either in soul or in body, and are not our own masters, we realize that, however irksome this truth may be, there is One stronger than ourselves, and that these favours are bestowed by Him, and that we, of ourselves, can do absolutely nothing. This imprints in us great humility. Indeed, I confess that in me it produced great fear—at first a terrible fear. One sees one's body being lifted up from the ground; and although the spirit draws it after itself, and if no resistance is offered does so very gently, one does not lose consciousness—at least, I myself have had sufficient to enable me to realize that I was being lifted up. The majesty of Him Who can do this is manifested in such a way that the hair stands on end, and there is produced a great fear of offending so great a God, but a fear overpowered by the deepest love, newly enkindled, for One Who, as we see, has so deep a love for so loathsome a worm that He seems not to be satisfied by literally drawing the soul to Himself, but will also have

> the body, mortal though it is, and befouled as is its clay by all the offenses it has committed.[38]

Bishop Diego de Yepes knew her well and wrote one of her many early biographies. One time, after receiving Communion from him through the grille at the convent, she started to rise. The bishop recorded her pleas as she clutched at the bars to stop her ascent:

> Lord, for a thing of so little consequence as is my being bereft of this favour of Thine, do not permit a creature so vile as I am to be taken for a holy woman.[39]

There are similar anecdotes told by nuns who saw St. Teresa spontaneously levitate. After the events, she would order them to never to speak of it, but later, under obedience to higher authorities during the Church's investigation into her life, they described the incidents. For her part, St. Teresa was greatly embarrassed by her levitations and prayed that they would stop, and by all accounts they decreased greatly in her later life.

St. Joseph of Cupertino

Perhaps the most famous levitating saint is Joseph of Cupertino (1603–1663). Joseph had a very difficult childhood. Today he probably would have been diagnosed with a psychiatric disorder

[38] *The Life of Teresa of Jesus: The Autobiography of Teresa of Ávila*, trans. and ed. E. Allison Peers, from the critical edition of P. Silverio de Santa Teresa, C.D., 113; the book can be found on the website of the Carmelite Monks, http://www.carmelitemonks.org/Vocation/teresa_life.pdf

[39] Fray Diego de Yepes, *Vida de Santa Teresa de Jesus* (Toledo, 1530).

of some kind. He was apparently not intelligent and was given the nickname "the open mouth" because he so often stared into space with his mouth agape. Meanwhile, perhaps due to his limitations and others' response to them, he developed a bad temper. To make matters worse, his father died when Joseph was quite young, and his mother may have been abusive toward him.

Joseph wanted to join the Franciscans, but due to his lack of education, they would not take him. He was then accepted by the Capuchins on a trial basis, but they sent him away after eight months. His mother did not want him back home, so she asked her brother, a Franciscan monk, to take him as a servant at his monastery. Her brother agreed and assigned Joseph to care for livestock. Over time, Joseph's temper mellowed, and he started doing better with his work—well enough for the Franciscans to allow him to study to become a priest. He was ordained in 1628.

After his ordination, Joseph undertook many penances, including rigorous fasting, usually eating solid food only twice per week. Then he started going into spiritual ecstasies when he said Mass or looked at devotional statues. During these ecstasies, he often levitated a few inches to a few feet off the ground. His levitations were so frequent that people started coming to see him for entertainment; during the investigation of his cause for sainthood, authorities corroborated at least seventy occasions when he levitated in the presence of witnesses.

One notable example happened during a visit to Italy from the Spanish ambassador and his wife. The ambassador had visited Joseph in his monastic cell and was so impressed that he wanted to return with his wife. Joseph entered the church where the couple hoped to meet him and, upon seeing a statue of Mary, elevated ten feet into the air, flew over the crowd to the statue, prayed, flew back to the door, and returned home. The Church later took depositions from a number of people who were there that day, and their stories were consistent. There were many other instances that were investigated in a similar way, including one in front of Pope Urban VIII. He was in Rome with a minister general who was his superior. It was customary to kiss the pope's feet at the time, as a sign of homage to the Holy Father. When Joseph did so, he rose into the air and was able to come back down only when his superior ordered him to do so. Pope Urban VIII said that if Joseph died during the pope's lifetime, he would testify to the levitation that happened in his presence.

After a time, Joseph's levitations became a problem for the monastery. Some thought the episodes were demonic, and he was denounced for witchcraft and investigated by the Inquisition. They sent him to a monastery in Assisi for observation. He was ordered not to say public Masses and to cease public appearances altogether. But his levitations continued in the monastery, and he was soon relegated to his cell and not even allowed to eat with the other friars. Joseph used this isolation to draw closer to God in prayer. Eventually the inquisition determined that he was not practicing witchcraft and let him return to regular monastic life. Joseph of Cupertino died in 1663 at the age of sixty and was canonized in 1767 by Pope Clement XIII.

St. Mary of Jesus Crucified

A more recent example of levitation is St. Mary of Jesus Crucified (1846–1878), who was canonized on May 17, 2015, by Pope Francis. Her life story was covered in the chapter on healings.

On June 22, 1873, the saint was missing at supper, and her fellow nuns went looking for her. They found her balanced on top of a large lime tree, singing. The mistress of novices ordered her to come down without hurting herself, and she complied immediately, lighting touching branches with her feet as she floated gently to the ground. The nuns documented seven more occasions when she levitated. As usual in these cases, some suspected her of trickery, so they spied on and watched her, but no natural explanation could be discovered.

Later a nun testified of the lime-tree incident, "She had taken hold of the tip of a little branch that a bird would have bent; and from there, in an instant, she had been lifted on high." A priest wrote to the local bishop about the levitations:

> Sister Mary used to raise herself to the top of the trees by the tips of the branches: she would take her scapular in one hand, and with the other the end of a small branch next to the leaves, and after a few moments she would glide along the outside edge of the tree to its top. Once up there, she would remain holding on to branches normally too weak to bear a person of her weight.[40]

Conclusions

There's a wonderful innocence, even childlikeness, in the stories of Sr. Mary's levitations. She would casually swing from branch to branch, all while singing of God's love. By the end of her life, witnesses reliably attested to eight such episodes, all in the courtyard of her monastery. We can see how a simple, faithful love of God can sometimes cause us to overcome our limitations. Usually this happens interiorly through the conversion of our

[40] Amedee Brunot, *Mariam, the Little Arab: Sister Mary of Jesus Crucified (1846–1878)* (Eugene, OR: Carmel of Maria Regina, 1984).

souls by grace, but sometimes, in extraordinary circumstances, it can happen outwardly through our bodies.

What purpose might God have in causing some ecstatics to levitate during prayer or praise of God? These levitations may prefigure the rising of the living at the second coming of Christ, detailed in 1 Thessalonians:

> For the Lord himself, with a word of command, with the voice of an archangel and with the trumpet of God, will come down from heaven, and the dead in Christ will rise first. Then we who are alive, who are left, will be caught up together with them in the clouds to meet the Lord in the air. Thus we shall always be with the Lord. (1 Thess. 4:16–17)

One could also see levitation as symbolic of rising above the corrupted world, rising above sin when entering a profound contemplation of God that pulls the spirit heavenward. Levitation is a very concrete miracle that serves as a sign of union with God, and calls the witnesses to seek the same.

8

Eucharistic Miracles

Theology of the Eucharist

The sixth chapter of the Gospel of John is important because in it we see the public starting to recognize who Jesus was. It begins with the story of the miracle of the loaves and the fishes which concludes with the following:

> When the people saw the sign he had done, they said, "This is truly the Prophet, the one who is to come into the world." (v. 14)

Jesus then withdrew from the crowd because He knew they wanted to carry him off and declare Him king before the right time. More importantly, He knew they believed in Him because He provided regular food, and not yet because of the spiritual food they really needed. Later that evening, the disciples saw Him walking on the water of the sea of Galilee, another miracle just for them to prepare them for the hard teachings He was about to give. They all arrived at Capernaum, and the people Jesus had fed arrived, looking for Him. They wanted another sign, but instead He told them some things that shocked them:

> I am the bread of life; whoever comes to me will never hunger, and whoever believes in me will never thirst. (v. 35)

And a bit later:

> I am the living bread that came down from heaven; whoever eats this bread will live forever; and the bread that I will give is my flesh for the life of the world. (v. 51)

When Christ's listeners murmured and argued about what this could possibly mean, He clarified:

> Jesus said to them, "Amen, amen, I say to you, unless you eat the flesh of the Son of Man and drink his blood, you do not have life within you. Whoever eats my flesh and drinks my blood has eternal life, and I will raise him on the last day. For my flesh is true food, and my blood is true drink. Whoever eats my flesh and drinks my blood remains in me and I in him. Just as the living Father sent me and I have life because of the Father, so also the one who feeds on me will have life because of me. This is the bread that came down from heaven. Unlike your ancestors who ate and still died, whoever eats this bread will live forever." (vv. 53–58)

This is the Bread of Life Discourse, one of the most dramatic moments in the Gospels. It is the foundation, along with the Last Supper, of the Church's teaching that the Eucharist is truly the Body and Blood of Christ. In the Upper Room on that last day with His apostles, Christ offered the meal and sacrifice that we celebrate at Mass to this day:

> When the hour came, he took his place at table with the apostles. He said to them, "I have eagerly desired to eat this Passover with you before I suffer, for, I tell you, I shall not eat it [again] until there is fulfillment in the

> kingdom of God." Then he took a cup, gave thanks, and said, "Take this and share it among yourselves; for I tell you [that] from this time on I shall not drink of the fruit of the vine until the kingdom of God comes." Then he took the bread, said the blessing, broke it, and gave it to them, saying, "This is my body, which will be given for you; do this in memory of me." And likewise the cup after they had eaten, saying, "This cup is the new covenant in my blood, which will be shed for you." (Luke 22:14–20)

The words of Christ are clear: the bread *is* His physical body, and the wine *is* His physical blood. And this is how the first Christians, including St. Paul, understood it:

> For I received from the Lord what I also handed on to you, that the Lord Jesus, on the night he was handed over, took bread, and, after he had given thanks, broke it and said, "This is my body that is for you. Do this in remembrance of me." In the same way also the cup, after supper, saying, "This cup is the new covenant in my blood. Do this, as often as you drink it, in remembrance of me." For as often as you eat this bread and drink the cup, you proclaim the death of the Lord until he comes. Therefore whoever eats the bread or drinks the cup of the Lord unworthily will have to answer for the body and blood of the Lord. A person should examine himself, and so eat the bread and drink the cup. For anyone who eats and drinks without discerning the body, eats and drinks judgment on himself. (1 Cor. 11:23–29)

Belief in the Real Presence of Christ in the Eucharist is therefore as ancient as the Church herself. The Church Fathers thought and wrote about it as if it were a given. In 1215, the term *transubstantiation* was incorporated into the Church dogma by the Fourth Lateran Council. We see this in canon 1:

> There is indeed one universal church of the faithful, outside of which nobody at all is saved, in which Jesus Christ is both priest and sacrifice. His body and blood are truly contained in the sacrament of the altar under the forms of bread and wine, the bread and wine having been changed in substance, by God's power, into his body and blood, so that in order to achieve this mystery of unity we receive from God what he received from us. Nobody can effect this sacrament except a priest who has been properly ordained according to the church's keys, which Jesus Christ himself gave to the apostles and their successors. But the sacrament of baptism is consecrated in water at the invocation of the undivided Trinity—namely Father, Son and holy Spirit—and brings salvation to both children and adults when it is correctly carried out by anyone in the form laid down by the church. If someone falls into sin after having received baptism, he or she can always be restored through true penitence. For not only virgins and the continent but also married persons find favour with God by right faith and good actions and deserve to attain to eternal blessedness.[41]

Three centuries later, this was reaffirmed at the Council of Trent (1545–1563) in session 13, chapter 4:

> And because that Christ, our Redeemer, declared that which He offered under the species of bread to be truly

[41] "Fourth Lateran Council: 1215," Papal Encyclicals Online, https://www.papalencyclicals.net/councils/ecum12-2.htm.

> His own body, therefore has it ever been a firm belief in the Church of God, and this holy Synod doth now declare it anew, that, by the consecration of the bread and of the wine, a conversion is made of the whole substance of the bread into the substance of the body of Christ our Lord, and of the whole substance of the wine into the substance of His blood; which conversion is, by the holy Catholic Church, suitably and properly called Transubstantiation.[42]

Finally, in the modern era, Pope St. Paul VI spoke of transubstantiation in his encyclical *Mysterium Fidei* in 1965:

> To avoid any misunderstanding of this type of presence, which goes beyond the laws of nature and constitutes the greatest miracle of its kind, we have to listen with docility to the voice of the teaching and praying Church. Her voice, which constantly echoes the voice of Christ, assures us that the way in which Christ becomes present in this Sacrament is through the conversion of the whole substance of the bread into His body and of the whole substance of the wine into His blood, a unique and truly wonderful conversion that the Catholic Church fittingly and properly calls transubstantiation. As a result of transubstantiation, the species of bread and wine undoubtedly take on a new signification and a new finality, for they are no longer ordinary bread and wine but instead a sign of something sacred and a sign of spiritual food; but they take on this new signification, this new finality, precisely

42 "General Council of Trent: Thirteenth Session," Papal Encyclicals Online, https://www.papalencyclicals.net/councils/trent/thirteenth-session.htm

> because they contain a new "reality" which we can rightly call ontological. For what now lies beneath the aforementioned species is not what was there before, but something completely different; and not just in the estimation of Church belief but in reality, since once the substance or nature of the bread and wine has been changed into the body and blood of Christ, nothing remains of the bread and the wine except for the species—beneath which Christ is present whole and entire in His physical "reality," corporeally present, although not in the manner in which bodies are in a place.[43]

In philosophy, we speak of the *substance* of a thing and the *accidents*, or appearance, of that thing. Your substance is yourself, your nature, what constitutes your identity. Your accidental traits, such as whether you wear your hair long or short, do not change your substance. When we say that the bread and wine have become transubstantiated, we are saying that the substance of the bread and wine have completely changed to become the Body, Blood, Soul, and Divinity of Jesus. The accidents of the bread and the wine, such as their appearance and taste, are not normally changed. Though transubstantiation during each Mass is a miracle in itself, when we say "Eucharistic miracle," we usually mean something related to the changing of the accidental traits of the bread or wine along with the invisible substance, which always changes at the Consecration.

The Real Presence Eucharistic Education and Adoration Association, in cooperation with the Pontifical Academy Cultorum

[43] Pope Paul VI, encyclical *Mysterium Fidei* (September 3, 1965), no. 46.

Martyrum, has published the book *The Eucharistic Miracles of the World*. This book is a companion to their traveling exhibition about 152 Eucharistic miracles from around the world that have been recognized by the Church. One can view the summaries of all the cases, organized by country, on the association's website.[44]

Eucharistic miracles, then, are affirmations of what Christ told us and of what the Church has always known. There have been many through the years, but two stand out because of the modern scientific analysis they were subjected to.

Lanciano

In the year 750, in Lanciano, Italy, then named Anxanum, a monastic priest who had doubts about the Real Presence of Jesus in the Eucharist was saying Mass in the monastery of Longinus. As he said the words of consecration, the bread and wine were transformed in their physical appearances into flesh and blood. The host became what looked like a slice of a human heart, and the wine coagulated into what looked like lumps of dried blood. The sacred species were set aside due to the miraculous event.

In 1970, the Franciscans of Lanciano sought an authoritative examination of the relics. In 1971, they chose Dr. Edoardo Linoli to do the analysis. Dr. Linoli was a professor of anatomy and pathological histology, as well as of chemistry and clinical microscopy. He was assisted by Dr. Ruggero Bertelli, a retired professor of anatomy. They found that the flesh was human cardiac

[44] *The Eucharistic Miracles of the World: Catalogue Book of the Vatican International Exhibition*, Real Presence Eucharistic Education and Adoration Association, http://www.therealpresence.org/eucharst/mir/engl_mir.htm.

tissue, specifically the endocardium (the membrane that lines the inside of the heart and valves). The blood type was AB. The findings were published in 1971.[45]

Buenos Aires

In 1996 in Buenos Aires, Argentina, another such even took place—and this time an investigation was able to occur in a timely manner. Everyone involved was interviewed on video, and experts were brought in right away. The story begins, however, on a disturbing note: on Sunday, August 18, 1996, at about 7:00 p.m., a consecrated host was found discarded in the parish church of Santa Maria.

When such a host is found, it is normally consumed by the priest unless it has been dirtied in some way. In this case, the host had been left on a dusty candleholder. The procedure in such cases is to let the host dissolve in a glass of water for a few days and then pour the water into an appropriate dignified place, usually the church's sacrarium, which is a sink with a pipe that goes directly into the earth. The Eucharist normally completely dissolves in the water, at which point it has lost the quality of "breadness" that had made it truly the Body of Christ, and it can be disposed of without sacrilege.

The parish priest in Buenos Aires left the host in a bowl of water in the tabernacle for eight days. When he checked on it, however, he was shocked to find not only an intact host, but what looked like blood on it. The priest locked the bowl in a tabernacle in his home where nobody else had access to it and

[45] *Quaderni Sclavo di Diagnostica Clinica e di Laboratori* 7, no. 3 (September 1971): 661–674.

then contacted his archbishop—Jorge Bergoglio, now Pope Francis—to ask for instructions. The archbishop told him to have the material professionally photographed and then to wait and see what happened. After the photography, the host was transferred to a test tube with distilled water to prevent contamination, where it remained for three years.

Archbishop Bergoglio then ordered that the material be investigated by an independent medical expert. Dr. Ricardo Castanon Gomez performed an initial examination in 1999 and concluded that the transformed host had all the characteristics of cardiac tissue, but the Argentinian doctor wanted to find an international expert to analyze the specimen. Five years later, a sample was taken to New York to be analyzed by Dr. Frederick Zugibe, a prominent forensic pathologist and expert on the heart. Importantly to the objectivity of the analysis, no one told Zugibe where the sample had come from. The entire analysis was recorded on video, which can be watched on the Internet.[46] This is part of what he said before he was told where the sample came from:

> The analyzed material is a fragment of the heart muscle found in the wall of the left ventricle close to the valves. This muscle is responsible for the contraction of the heart. It should be borne in mind that the left cardiac ventricle pumps blood to all parts of the body. The heart muscle is in an inflammatory condition and contains a large number of white blood cells. This indicates that the heart was alive at the time the sample was taken. It is my

[46] "Blood of Christ Part 1: The Eucharistic Miracle of Buenos Aires," YouTube video, 34:06, posted by Reason to Believe, August 29, 2019, https://www.youtube.com/watch?v=bd16tBRbLXw.

> contention that the heart was alive, since white blood cells die outside a living organism. They require a living organism to sustain them. Thus, their presence indicates that the heart was alive when the sample was taken. What is more, these white blood cells had penetrated the tissue, which further indicates that the heart had been under severe stress, as if the owner had been beaten severely about the chest.

Meanwhile the blood type, as in Lanciano, was found to be AB. This is also the blood type found in the blood on the Shroud of Turin. Three attempts were made by different labs to do a genetic analysis of the blood, but DNA could not be extracted even though intact white blood cells were present. As DNA techniques advance, there may be additional attempts to analyze the DNA of the blood.

A Potential Miracle in America

On October 7, 2016, the Diocese of Youngstown, Ohio, opened the cause for the canonization of Rhoda Wise, a mystic and stigmatic who lived in Canton. During her life, Rhoda's modest home became a pilgrimage location for those seeking wisdom and healings. She was said to be able to speak face-to-face with Jesus Christ, as He would come and sit next to her bed and talk with her. Later in life, she experienced dramatic stigmata wounds. One of the people who came to Rhoda for advice and healing was a young woman from across Canton named Rita Rizzo. She went on to credit Rhoda and the intercession of St. Thérèse of Lisieux for miraculous relief from a debilitating stomach ailment. Rita Rizzo is better known as Mother Angelica, foundress of the

Eternal Word Television Network (EWTN). Rhoda Wise died in 1948 at the age of sixty.

When I visited the Rhoda Wise home, I was directed to an apparent Eucharistic miracle. There is a large bottle of holy water that was apparently blessed by Jesus Himself, with the promise that it would heal many. This water is topped off on a regular basis so that it never runs out. Years ago, a previous custodian of the house was filling the small holy water bottles given away to pilgrims when there was a flash of light. When she regained her focus, the custodian saw a host floating in the large bottle of water. It had not been dropped into the water, and there had been no hosts nearby. The host has never dissolved in the subsequent decades and can still be seen resting at the bottom of the bottle, looking just like a typical host you would receive at Mass. This potential miracle has not yet been validated by the Church, but perhaps an investigation will someday occur as part of Rhoda Wise's cause.[47]

My Own Story

What I am about to share is a personal experience, one that I do not claim to be a miracle—and yet it made apparent the reality of the Eucharist for me in a tangible way. During a pilgrimage to the Holy Land, I attended Mass in the Moses Chapel of the church on Mount Hermon—the Mount of Transfiguration. When I received Communion, at first everything was normal: I received on the tongue and closed my mouth. Instead of the normal round host I had received, I felt a large, irregularly shaped, and very soft substance lying across most of my tongue. In the next moment,

[47] See The Rhoda Wise Story, https://rhodawise.com/.

as fast as the snap of a finger, my mouth was filled with fluid such that I worried it would spill out between my lips. I tasted nothing, and I certainly did not chew. Though I was alarmed, I didn't want to distract others, so I made no gesture or sound. Later I talked with the priest to confirm that there was nothing unusual about the hosts used at Mass, and there was not.

I will never know—until Heaven, God willing—what happened that day. I can assure you that there is no special holiness in me that would merit such a sign. More likely, it was a kind of confirmation given to me in my weakness—perhaps related to my work training exorcists. It is also possible that it was given for this book. Regardless of why it happened, I know that I will never forget that day. I knew from attending hundreds of exorcisms that Jesus is alive and present everywhere and at all times, but He is present in a special way in the Eucharist. That day gave me additional proof of His Real Presence and love for all of us in the Mass. I suspect that there are many such experiences that occur, but we never hear about them.

Conclusions

For the Catholic, Eucharistic miracles are perhaps the most direct indicators of the reality of God. They confirm what Jesus said and what Scripture and the Church testify to. They also draw us personally to a deeper appreciation for the God who lowers Himself to meet us in a physical way while we are on our earthly pilgrimage. Eucharistic miracles are also potent and, like Christ's teaching so many years ago on consuming His Flesh and Blood, can overwhelm us.

The reality of the Body and Blood of Jesus is normally veiled behind the bread and wine. This reality is a mystery; it is not simply that the bread *really is* heart tissue. Rather, the heart tissue reminds us of the love of Jesus that He feels in His heart, given to each of us at every Communion. And the blood reminds us of what He shed to cleanse our sins and open the way to Heaven for us.

9

Misunderstood Mental Illness

When we hear about a miracle, our first reaction — not necessarily wrongly — is to question the reliability of the source. This is especially true in cases that rely only on personal testimony. What do those persons have to gain? Are they just seeking attention? Maybe they're naive, melodramatic, or simply mistaken. Maybe they are mentally ill.

Discerning the difference between supernatural events, demonic counterfeits, and mental illness is one of the most important things I do. It is important so that the person who has had the experience can be treated properly. It is also important for those around the person, so that they can learn how to respond to what is going on. Let's begin with a brief overview of mental illness.

Broadly speaking, we can divide the mentally ill into two categories: those who can adequately function in society and those who cannot. We generally do not encounter those in the latter category, the seriously mentally ill, in public. In the past, they would live in state hospitals or asylums; today, after the closure of so many mental health facilities, they often end up living in prison. It is common for the seriously mentally ill to claim all kinds of unusual experiences, but their illnesses are so pronounced that their claims are dismissed out of hand. They may have genuine supernatural experiences, but it would be very hard to separate such experiences from hallucination or delusion.

Mild to moderate mental illness goes from run-of-the-mill anxiety and depression to more serious, but treatable, disorders. Those who suffer from such illnesses are generally able to go to work, to maintain relationships, and to take care of themselves in society. Many forms of mental illness worsen with increased stress and age, and some can get dramatically worse quickly, such as the side effects of a tumor.

Perhaps the most notable form of mental illness for our purposes is schizophrenia, which is a progressive disease that changes the physical structure of the brain. Generally, the person with schizophrenia struggles socially while growing up, then has an abrupt and dramatic onset of symptoms called a "psychotic break." This break often happens in a person's twenties or thirties at a time of increased stress, such as when starting a first job, when getting married, or during another big life change. One of the main symptoms of schizophrenia is persistent auditory hallucinations—hearing voices. These usually seem to come from outside of the person, but they can also seem to be in the mind. Visual hallucinations can occur but are much less common.

It is very common for people with schizophrenia to apply their spiritual worldview to the voices they hear, often interpreting them as being from God or the devil. This is how they try to make sense of an experience they are having. Those raised Christian might call the voices demons or Jesus; those raised Muslim might call them djinn; those raised Buddhist might call them animal spirits; and so on. It is important to understand that, *to the schizophrenics*, these experiences feel absolutely true. To them, the voices are as real as any experience you have had;

there is no doubt that they are real. Their only doubt is how to explain them and deal with them.

A delusion is a fixed idea that is not rational and does not respond to rational challenge. Generally, the delusion is impervious to challenge. To someone who thinks the CIA is out to get him, everyone who assures him otherwise looks like an agent. This kind of persistent, self-protective delusion is what is called a thought disorder, and it is part of a number of mental illnesses, but it is mostly seen with schizophrenia. The combination of the voices with delusional ideas about the world leads many schizophrenics to think they are possessed or that God is talking to them. It is common for them to call the church to request an exorcism, which, of course, is denied.

It can be difficult to distinguish between mental illness and mysticism. The mentally ill may claim to be hearing from God, as do genuine mystics. Both are sincere in their beliefs. The first commonsense difference is that mystics think and function in an otherwise normal way. They usually have an accurate perspective on how their experiences seem to other people, and they usually have no desire to be known or to share their experiences with others. They function well in life and are able to do what they need to do. The genuinely mentally ill usually have other mental health problems manifesting in their lives, and they are often disorganized, confused, depressed, or generally not able to take care of themselves. A history of mental health treatment, medications, or inpatient stays also points away from genuine mysticism.

The second criteria that the Church uses to discern if mysticism is genuine is whether the private revelations are in line with Church teaching. A good example is Mary of Agreda's (1602–1665) *Mystical City of God.* This work is 2,676 pages of background stories behind many events in the Bible, and nothing in it was found to be out of line with Church teaching. This four-volume book was dictated to Venerable Mother Mary of Jesus of Agreda by Mary the Mother of God. She wrote it down only under obedience, and she did not want people to know about her mystical experiences with Mary. The material in these books is private revelation, but it has received an imprimatur by several popes and bishops (a kind of seal saying there is no error in it) as well as the nihil obstat (a declaration that it is inoffensive to faith or morals). She submitted her writing to the authority of the Church and allowed the Church to determine whether the material was free of error.

In contrast, the mentally ill often have strange ideas in their theology and are completely opposed to correction, since delusional ideas are fixed, rigid, and resistant to challenge. When groups of people have followed material that arose from mental illness, it has almost always led to a break away from the Church and to the self-destruction of the group within a few months or years. The mentally ill person wants the world to conform to his ideas; the genuine mystic wants to conform himself to Christ's Church.

When delusions are combined with charisma, as we will see in chapter 11, the situation can become dangerous. Given the right circumstances, charismatic delusional people may attract others who believe them without question and soon become just as much a slave to the delusions as the leaders themselves. These groups usually evolve into increasingly apocalyptic forms and crash.

A Historic Fascination with Mental Illness and Possession

One interesting story at the origin of modern psychology combined a brilliant charismatic doctor with potential demonic activity. Jean-Martin Charcot (1825–1893) is regarded as the founder of neurology, and his name is connected to a number of disorders that he identified, such as Charcot-Marie-Tooth disease. He is best known for his work with what was in his time was called "hysteria."

The ideas of animal magnetism and mesmerism were popular in Charcot's day. These posited that there is an invisible field among all living things that can be manipulated by people or magnetic materials. Franz Mesmer (1734–1815) had popularized these ideas, and Charcot developed Mesmer's techniques with women who exhibited hysteria. These women would exhibit strange body contortions, respond to hallucinations, and sometimes take rigid poses for hours. Charcot was the first to develop hypnosis from working with these women, and with it he could induce the altered states, contortions, and strange experiences. Charcot ran the largest psychiatric hospital in Paris, the Salpêtrière, so he had access to many patients. The hospital had been in operation since the 1600s, and it mainly housed women (in 1690 there were already three thousand women confined there).[48]

Charcot's most famous patient was Louise Augustine Gleizes, or simply Augustine. She was an attractive girl from Paris who would exhibit dramatic contortions and strange experiences when subjected to Charcot's version of hypnosis. She had been subjected to abuse and rape at an early age and confined to the hospital at the age of fourteen. Her hysterical episodes would be induced as demonstrations for visiting doctors from all over Europe. One of those doctors was Sigmund Freud, who was greatly

[48] For the entire story please see *The Invention of Hysteria: Charcot and the Photographic Iconography of the Salpêtrière* (Cambridge, MA: MIT Press, 2004).

impressed, so much so that a painting of one such demonstration hung over his desk during the years when he developed psychoanalysis. Photography had also just been invented, and many images were captured of the various patients in their contorted states and experiencing hallucinations.

What is less well known about Charcot is that he had an abiding interest in the history of spiritual possession. He had in his home a small museum of images of possession states, and a number of the images taken of Augustine are described as the process of interaction with an "infernal husband."[49] Many of the details of the displays exhibited for the visiting doctors would be scandalous to the modern reader. At the intersection of hypnosis, sexual post-traumatic stress disorder (PTSD), and a doctor fascinated with the idea of possession, many disturbing behaviors can be imagined. Whether there were genuine demonic spirits involved cannot be known. There are striking similarities, however, between some of the images and the physical contortions seen in contemporary exorcisms.

We also know that demonic spirits are very comfortable with demoniacs' going to psychologists or mental health hospitals. They do not find these treatments threatening, and so they prefer the person be treated only as mentally ill. This emphasizes the great importance of cooperation between medicine and the ministry of exorcism, which the Church has long identified as essential.

The Church has forbidden engaging in hypnosis, as it is a submission of the will to another. We read in the Vatican document *Jesus Christ: The Bearer of the Water of Life—A Reflection on the "New Age"*:

[49] Ibid., 146.

> "The point of *New Age* techniques is to reproduce mystical states at will, as if it were a matter of laboratory material. Rebirth, biofeedback, sensory isolation, holotropic breathing, hypnosis, mantras, fasting, sleep deprivation and transcendental meditation are attempts to control these states and to experience them continuously". These practices all create an atmosphere of psychic weakness (and vulnerability).[50]

A final observation: if a therapist tries to hypnotize a possessed person, the demonic spirits immediately interrupt the hypnosis process and challenge the therapist. The spirits also do not respond to attempts to bring the person back to his normal senses. Hypnosis seems to weaken the will of the person, leaving the body more easily animated by the possessing spirits. This reinforces the Church's conclusion and judgment about hypnosis as a technique that weakens the psyche.

Conclusions

There is no simple formula for distinguishing between spiritual experiences and mental illness. There are also milder forms of mental illness that can be hard to detect but that affect the person. This is why the Church is slow to render judgment on claims of miracles or supernatural events. Time often reveals whether people are stable or unstable, sane or mentally ill.

[50] Pontifical Council for Culture, Pontifical Council for Interreligious Dialogue, *Jesus Christ the Bearer of the Water of Life: A Christian Reflection on the "New Age,"* 4, quoting Michel Lacroix, *L'Ideologia della New Age* (Milan: Il Saggiatore, 1998), 74.

When people approach the Church requesting an exorcism, the first step is to rule out medical and mental illness. This is because most cases are not spiritual but are mundane. If the Church too quickly believed claims of miracles or demons, people would not be served well but could be reinforced in delusional beliefs that do harm to them. Only after ensuring that a person is sane and healthy, and the signs of possession exist, does the Church endorse the idea of possession and allow an exorcism. Likewise, when a claim of a miracle is made, one of the questions is the sanity of the claimant.

10

Demonic Counterfeits

Not every false miracle has a natural explanation. There are things that go beyond nature that are not from God: these are demonic counterfeits. The Church has always been aware of this and has generally been careful not to rule extraordinary happenings to be of divine origin too quickly. It is important to understand that nothing that the devil does is a miracle, even if it seems to, and sometimes does, break the rules of nature. A miracle by definition is *supernatural*, or above nature. The things the devil does are merely *preternatural*, or beside nature. The devil's antics are not miracles that go beyond created reality but are a manipulation of the reality that God has already created.

In the work of exorcism, we see many of the antics of demons, and some things seem to be clear. The first is that demons cannot create. A demon can move things from here to there, sometimes apparently instantly, but it cannot create something from nothing. Only God can create. Usually we see this in extraordinary demonic cases, such as infestation, oppression, and possession, and not merely in temptations or lesser oppression.[51] Examples

[51] Demonic infestation is when a demon has gained the right to do extraordinary things in a place. Demonic oppression is

include making holy objects disappear in the home of a possessed person, making a person seem to cough up nails or other metal objects, causing unlikely car accidents, and hiding important personal property to annoy a person.

The second thing we see in the antics of demons is that demons can only look at what God does and perform a distorted counterfeit of that. The demon does nothing genuinely new. This is why there are demonic versions of most of the genuine miracles we have been discussing. A demon can seem to heal a person, but it is either the removal of a malady that the demon caused or the masking of symptoms. A demon can make a false image that claims to be a ghost, or Mary, or St. Michael, or even Jesus. In such cases, there always seems to be something missing, hidden, or deformed. The two tips that a "ghost" is a demon are that and when they want to have a conversation. The poor souls in Purgatory do not draw people into necromancy.[52] Demons can cause real wounds in possessed people's flesh, which is sometimes a mockery of stigmata. Finally, in possessed people, demons rarely cause levitation, either a few inches off the floor or many feet or yards.

The third thing we see in demonic activity is that demons need permission from God for everything they do, as in the book of Job (1:6–12). It is important to remember that a demon, though capable of deceptive tricks, is continuously restrained by God. The

---

when a demon has gained the right to attack a person in an extraordinary way. Demonic possession is when a demon has gained the right to take over a person's lower faculties: his body and his emotions.

[52] For more on this demonic trick and "ghost hunting," see my book *Hauntings, Possessions, and Exorcisms* (Steubenville, OH: Emmaus Road Publishing, 2017).

demon is not running free, doing whatever he wishes. It is usually through their own free will that people give license to demons to act in their lives and in areas over which they have authority. This is usually done through violations of the first commandment: putting something before God and turn to it for comfort, information, or power. This is why the occult, magic (not sleight of hand), and recourse to psychics are so strongly forbidden in the Bible and in Church teaching. When we break our relationship with God and start a new relationship with a spirit that we make requests of, we give that spirit rights to enter our lives.

Spiritualism and Necromancy in Scripture

Spiritualism, which is the attempt to consult spirits for hidden truths, consolations, or predictions, is nothing new. In biblical times, it was a common practice in many cultures. The words most commonly used in the Bible for this practice are *necromancy* and *sorcery*, which in the ancient world meant a few things: asking for favors, taking revenge on enemies, and performing acts that are beyond human capability. This was usually accomplished with the help of a "medium" or a "sorcerer" who claimed to be able to facilitate communication with spirits and so to perform "black magic." The Old Testament took a very negative view of these practices, which not only directed people's devotion away from the Lord but almost always involved bad motives:

> Do not turn to ghosts or consult spirits, by which you will be defiled. I, the LORD, am your God. (Lev. 19:31)

> Should anyone turn to ghosts and spirits and prostitute oneself with them, I will turn against that person and cut such a one off from among the people. (Lev. 20:6)

> Let there not be found among you anyone who causes their son or daughter to pass through the fire, or practices divination, or is a soothsayer, augur, or sorcerer, or who casts spells, consults ghosts and spirits, or seeks oracles from the dead. Anyone who does such things is an abomination to the Lord, and because of such abominations the LORD, your God, is dispossessing them before you. You must be altogether sincere with the LORD, your God. (Deut. 18:10–13)

> Thus Saul died because of his treason against the LORD in disobeying his word, and also because he had sought counsel from a ghost, rather than from the LORD. Therefore the LORD took his life, and turned his kingdom over to David, the son of Jesse. (1 Chron. 10:13–14)

These admonitions are not limited to the Old Testament: The New Testament also addresses spiritualism in a number of places:

> Now the works of the flesh are obvious: immorality, impurity, licentiousness, idolatry, sorcery, hatreds, rivalry, jealousy, outbursts of fury, acts of selfishness, dissensions, factions, occasions of envy, drinking bouts, orgies, and the like. I warn you, as I warned you before, that those who do such things will not inherit the kingdom of God. (Gal. 5:19–21)

> Now the Spirit explicitly says that in the last times some will turn away from the faith by paying attention to deceitful spirits and demonic instructions through the hypocrisy of liars with branded consciences. (1 Tim. 4:1–2)

> But as for cowards, the unfaithful, the depraved, murderers, the unchaste, sorcerers, idol-worshipers, and deceivers

> of every sort, their lot is in the burning pool of fire and sulfur, which is the second death. (Rev. 21:8)
>
> Outside are the dogs, the sorcerers, the unchaste, the murderers, the idol-worshipers, and all who love and practice deceit. (Rev. 22:15)

When people turn to spirits other than God for information, comfort, or power, they are breaking the first commandment: they are breaking their friendship with God and starting a relationship with the enemies of God. It is no wonder, then, that almost all extraordinary demonic problems people encounter have a violation of the first commandment as their source.

Spiritualism in Modern History

As in biblical times, people today are fascinated with the idea of spirits that can satisfy our desires for power, revenge, consolation, or pleasure. Modern spiritualism can be traced to Hydesville, New York, in 1848. Two young girls, ten-year-old Catherine and fourteen-year-old Margaretta Fox, claimed to hear knocking noises in their house that would answer questions intelligently. They would ask a question, and observers would hear either one or two knocks that were meant to mean yes or no. The girls could reproduce this phenomenon for witnesses, and they became internationally famous.

This initiated a wave of interest in conjuring spirits across the Western world. Séances with mediums became popular family activities in many homes in the era before radio and television. It was such a mainstream activity that Carl Jung wrote his doctoral dissertation on séances performed by his cousin, who claimed to be a medium.

This growing cultural interest in spiritualism and parapsychology—the study of psychic phenomena—led to the founding of the Society for Psychical Research (SPR) in the United Kingdom in 1882. The SPR was funded by wealthy members with an interest in the paranormal, but over time, more and more hoaxes, tricks, and lies were exposed. Harry Houdini, the famous magician, did a great amount of work exposing the tricks of the physical mediums who claimed to produce "ectoplasm" and other phenomena. Toward the end of the nineteenth century, Arthur Conan Doyle, author of the Sherlock Holmes stories, led a mass resignation of most of the members of the SPR.

Around that time, in 1888, Margaretta Fox admitted her and her sister's hoax and described how they had created the noises back in 1848:

> When we went to bed at night we used to tie an apple to a string and move the string up and down, causing the apple to bump on the floor, or we would drop the apple on the floor, making a strange noise every time it would rebound. Mother listened to this for a time. She would not understand it and did not suspect us as being capable of a trick because we were so young.

There was a bit of a lull in interest in spiritualism after this, but it was far from dead. In 1891, the Ouija board, on which the user allows a pointer called a "planchette" to be "guided" to letters and numbers on the board that seem to spell out messages, received a patent, and soon families had a commercial tool with which to practice necromancy in their homes without the help of a hired medium. The first half of the twentieth century saw a resurgence in interest in spiritualism, as two world wars and a depression led to a great deal of spiritual confusion and fascination with the possibility of communicating with the dead.

Spiritualism ebbed again during the postwar years, until 1957 when the BBC televised an interview with Gerald Gardner, the founder of modern witchcraft (now called Wicca). This interview was a global sensation and led to many occult-themed movies in the 1960s and a renewed interest in witchcraft as a real modern practice, rather than just a historical footnote. This modern invention was called "witchcraft" by Gardner, and he called the people who practiced it "wiccans." It was a combination of the black magic of Aleister Crowley, Gardner's own inventions, and Freemasonry.

Finally, the modern wave of interest in the spirit world began in 2004 with the launch of the first paranormal reality show on cable television, which showed normal people using digital recorders, laser thermometers, and video cameras to document apparent ghosts. The show was so popular that dozens of similar shows have been created in subsequent years. These programs use modern technology to try to answer the same questions asked in previous generations: Are spirits real, and what can be gained from them?

I have known a number of the paranormal television celebrities. What Hollywood does not show is the impact of this kind of curiosity and experimentation with spiritualism on the people involved. Not all of the "professionals" in this field have trouble, but many do. One couple who specialized in electronic voice phenomena (EVP)—supposed ghost voices left on recordings—were very troubled in their home by spiritual manifestations such as noises, black shadows, and worse. The husband called me one morning and said, cryptically, "Do not judge me before everything is revealed," and then, "I guess the thing in the house is going to get what it wants." The next morning, September 22, 2015, he murdered his wife and her boyfriend and then killed himself in a standoff with police.

There are many other stories of broken families, strange illnesses, depression, and possession that have come from "paranormal investigation." These are hidden from the public since they aren't good for ratings or selling tickets to events. I spoke at paranormal conferences for years, warning people that spirit communication is dangerous because it amounts to talking with demons.

The deadly serious business of communicating with the spiritual enemies of God has been reduced to a game or a pastime that lures people in. There are Ouija board apps for smartphones and pink Ouija boards for toddlers in toy stores. There are starter kits for children to practice witchcraft. More recently, things have become more openly demonic: the paranormal television shows now explicitly use witchcraft, and there is a children's book on summoning demons called *A Children's Book of Demons*. What used to be masked as communicating with ghosts is now more openly framed as consorting with demons.

While most of the phenomena in the history of spiritualism has been faked, there have been instances of truly unexplainable events. These are almost always demons pretending to be some spirit or other, but because they appear to be beyond nature, we can be easily fooled into thinking their activities are authentic miracles. These shams, nonetheless, have seduced many people into the spiritual confusion of the "New Age," or the more honest areas of witchcraft and Satanism. These systems are most attractive to people who feel disempowered or traumatized by life, which is why one generally sees young troubled people in these groups. The essential message is the same as the one posited in the Garden of Eden: you can become like God. The promise is that by applying this hidden knowledge and practicing these methods, you can form a relationship with spirits that will give you what you want right now, on your own terms. Of course, demons only play along with this and pretend to be subservient to these methods—until the person is in too deep to back out. This is why we have so many cases of people asking the Church to help them after they use these systems.

One of the very successful tactics of demons who manifest as ghosts is to present themselves as lost loved ones, causing people to drop their guard and to engage in a relationship with them. In the beginning, the demon pretends to be either helpful or needy and pathetic. This most commonly takes the form of a little girl, sometimes one who appears to be sick. This is simply because females are generally less threatening than males, and children less threatening than adults. Finally, in the case of a female target, children activate women's maternal instincts and draw them in.

This tactic is most often used on the bereaved, particularly parents. Apparent "miraculous visions" of this kind are used to convince a person that this spirit is a loved one. The demon might even use a secret nickname or some other private piece information to demonstrate his genuineness. But this is only bait to draw in a vulnerable person, to gain his or her trust, and then to abuse that trust by drawing the victim away from the truth and from God. The initial interaction seems to give comfort under the pretense that the apparition is a lost loved one. In reality, this deepens the trauma and distress, as the person can no longer grieve and process the loss. A new disordered relationship forms with the sham, and then, over time, the demon starts to exhibit a bit more of its real nature by teaching lies about the spirit world, the afterlife, and theology. Then it starts dictating what the person can and cannot do. A whole generation of spiritualist books have emerged from these practices, which generally espouse the same generic New Age philosophies and theology.

A False Mystic: Sr. Magdalena of the Cross

One historical example of demons' creating a counterfeit mystic illustrates the danger of naively accepting claims of visions and miracles. It also illustrates why the Church, with hard-won wisdom, is slow to declare these phenomena divine or to declare a person a saint based on them.

Sr. Magdalena of the Cross was born in Spain in 1487 and became a Franciscan nun who was renowned across Spain and most of Europe. She was famous for the miracles that she apparently performed and for her extreme penances. She was called a living saint, and, like many genuine saints, she started having visions early in life—around five years old. She was praying in church, and a luminous young man appeared to her. When she described what she had seen, many thought it was Jesus who had appeared to her, and her fame started to spread. Later this same figure appeared to her and told her to lessen her penances in order to protect her health. After that, she helped a lame man up the stairs of the church, and he seemed to be spontaneously healed. Shortly thereafter, a mute person recovered his voice, apparently due to her power.

At the age of ten, there were indications that something was amiss. Magdalena tried to crucify herself to the wall of her bedroom as a penance for being a beautiful child. The wounds became infected, and then she claimed that Jesus had healed her. She then apparently fasted for three months leading up to her first Holy Communion, but when she approached to receive the Eucharist, she threw herself on the floor and later claimed that Jesus had given her the Eucharist Himself; thus she avoided actually receiving Him.

In spite of this, at the age of seventeen she became a Franciscan nun—but her behavior soon started to cause concern in the convent. She did extreme penances, sometimes carrying a heavy cross around, and seemed to stop eating completely. These types of displays—note that these were public penances, as opposed to the private penances of genuine saints—are generally not allowed in religious orders since they tend to distract the person and others from their proper responsibilities. Nonetheless, she was allowed to continue, and her reputation for saintliness grew.

When she made her perpetual vows in the Franciscan Order, many from far and wide were in attendance. A dove flew down from the ceiling of the cathedral and landed on her shoulder, then flew up and sat watching the ceremony. When the ceremony ended, it flew outside and straight up into the sky. This story spread far and wide, and again her fame increased. Due to Sr. Magdalena's reputation, many patrons donated a lot of money to the monastery.

As her life in the convent continued, she started to exhibit knowledge of things she could not have known: events in the city, in another Franciscan convent, and in the noble families. She started predicting the future, such as the deaths of political figures and the appointment of a cardinal. Then, on the feast of the Annunciation in 1518, she told her abbess that by the Holy Spirit she had conceived Jesus within herself the previous night. The abbess kept this a secret in order to wait and see what would happen, and Magdalena's belly soon started to show what seemed to be a pregnancy. The nuns were then told of their sister's claim, and controversy ensued; despite an order not to speak of the situation, word leaked to the outside world. Meanwhile, Magdalena increased her gruesome penances, including walking on broken glass and lashing herself.

When the archbishop heard of the sister's story, he sent three midwives to examine her. They determined both that she was indeed pregnant, and that her virginity was intact. She claimed that she would give birth on Christmas Eve 1518, and that she must do so alone. The nuns set up a little house for her, and she retreated there in solitude. When she emerged, she did not have a child, and told an outlandish story about the child's disappearing. But her sisters and devotees believed her, and again her fame only increased. More extraordinary events happened, and she was tested to ensure that her spiritual ecstasies were real and that she really was living without eating. The ecstasies were tested by seeing if she would respond to pain when in an ecstasy, which she did not. Observation to confirm she was not eating in her cell was done—but not well enough.

The money kept flowing in, and the monastery became the richest in Spain. The nuns helped to fund a new cathedral, which ingratiated the monastery to the archdiocese, and so Sr. Magdalena's influence increased further. In 1533, she was elected abbess and immediately became tyrannical, forcing the nuns to endure greater penances than they could bear and accusing them of greater sins than they confessed. This sent some of the nuns into hysterical fits that looked like temporary states of demonic possession. Then the abbess claimed that St. Francis had appeared to her and told her that they no longer needed to go to confession. Rather, she had her nuns confess nightly to her in her cell.

In spite of all this, her fame continued to spread in the outside world. Even Queen Isabella of Spain sent the abbess her portrait and asked for her prayers. Within the monastery, however, she was losing support due to her increasingly abusive behavior, and she was removed as abbess. Shortly thereafter, she became seriously ill and a priest came to hear her general confession in preparation for death. When he put the purple stole on her, she went into a suspicious "ecstasy." The priest suspected that this was a demonic response to the holy object, and he tested her with holy water, which caused her to lash out further. Then she started voicing blasphemies and floating in the air over her bed and violently dropping back down. The priest summoned an exorcist.

During the rite, it became clear that Magdalena had been possessed by two demons, one of whom reveled in the problems he had caused through her. In the end, though, the exorcism was successful. Later, an inquisitor came to investigate the case and to record the details. Sr. Magdalena was now near death, and she admitted that the young man who came to her when she was a girl was the devil and that he promised her fame and respect if she would obey him. She further admitted the demons encouraged and made possible all of her supposed revelations, fasting regimens, and ecstasies.

But the ordeal was not yet over. She again began vulgarly insulting the inquisitor, and further exorcisms expelled the second demon. Finally, she was completely freed from the possession that had enslaved her for forty years. She repented for the decades during which she had willfully cooperated with the demons. She lived out the rest of her days in penance and prayer, never exhibiting the disordered ideas or manifestations again.

The story of Sr. Magdalena shows how the devil can manifest extraordinary signs and experiences that, even to those who should know better, look like the holy works of God. But, on inspection, these are always distortions of true sanctity—precisely the kind of distortions that can pull people in and cause enormous damage. The demons who possessed Sr. Magdalena wanted to destroy all the goodness they could by drawing well-meaning people to her: her fellow nuns, powerful people, and the everyday faithful. And for a very long time, they succeeded. Besides the people whom Sr. Magdalena hurt personally, untold numbers more had their faith shaken by the revelation of her deception.

This is an example of why the Church regards all claims of supernatural experiences with careful scrutiny. Sr. Magdalena's story is extraordinary—thank God such events have not happened more often in the history of the Church—but it is a reminder to us, and to all spiritual authorities, to be vigilant.

Demonic False Apparitions at Lourdes

After the visions ended for St. Bernadette, a number of false apparitions occurred to other people at Lourdes, but these were from the devil and were designed to cast doubt on the valid apparitions. The first was a young woman who saw a different version of Mary holding a child she could not make out. She saw more instances of this apparition later, but without the child. The second was a woman struggling with alcoholism who saw the same image. The third was a prostitute, who again saw the same image. In the end, a total of thirty people reported seeing apparitions in the grotto after the visions to St. Bernadette ended. The true number was likely much larger, as they stopped recording the additional reports.

All of these false apparitions did not appear where Mary had appeared to St. Bernadette, but rather in a small tunnel in the wall on the opposite side of the cave. The tunnel was high on the wall and required the ladies to climb on the altar to access the tunnel. The apparition caused one of the women to break down in anxiety and distress. A well-known local lady recorded that one of the false visionaries tried to throw herself in the nearby river and drown herself after seeing the apparition. A priest who investigated these events recorded that some of the figures seen were reported as engaging in obscene gestures.

Several of the false visionaries would request rosaries but insisted that they not be blessed ones. They said that Jesus was going to pray the Rosary with the people. One of the false visionaries would go into convulsions and grind his teeth when he had a vision. Another boy started braying like a donkey and making horrific faces. All of these false apparitions almost succeeded in causing the investigating commission to render a negative decision about St. Bernadette's visions, which was likely the devil's intent.

Demonic Parlor Tricks

Demons are fallen angels; people who are damned do not become demons. When angels were created, they were each created for a purpose and given the ability to perform that purpose. This ability can be called a faculty. We see in Scripture that angels seem to have specific jobs they specialize in: Gabriel was a messenger, Raphael was a healer, and Michael was a warrior. In the beginning (as described in Revelation 9:1), a number of angels followed Satan and fell from heaven to earth. When they fell, they did not lose their specialties, but retained them in a kind of inverse. An angel who was created to inspire chastity would become a demon who inspires lust. Other fallen angels had faculties that were more physical, so one might encounter a demon who can make things move or bang with no apparent cause. I call these "parlor tricks" because that is what they are—manipulations of nature designed to trick us into fear or submission or to get us to back off.

The various manifestations demons perform have similarities to miraculous things that happen around saints or holy angels. This is no coincidence, again, as the fallen angels are just misusing the holy powers that God manifests through saints and holy angels. The fallen angels cannot do things they were not created to do; they can do only what they were created to do, but in a distorted way, as a plumber can use a wrench either to fix a pipe or loosen it so it will leak.

Here is a list of the parlor tricks that demons have been seen to produce, from common to less common:

- *Causing very bad odors that have no normal source.* These are usually a mix of terrible smells, and they move and are present only where the spirit is manifesting. This is an inversion of what we see with many saints, where a scent of beautiful flowers occurs. We also see the scent of flowers occurring with most stigmatics, specifically from the wounds.
- *Causing shadows that have no normal source.* These shadows are like a solid black mass of smoke that moves and rolls through the air. They are solid enough to prevent a person from seeing through them even in a well-lit room. They vary in size from a few inches to larger than a large man. This is an inversion of the light we sometimes see coming from saints, as well as the light seen coming from holy angels or apparitions of Mary.
- *Making noises and, rarely, talking.* Scratching or growling sounds in the walls or near a person is common in demonic cases. Investigations reveal no infestations of

animals. In rare cases, demons have talked audibly out of the air. This is an inversion of holy angels' ability to speak to people, which we see in a number of biblical accounts.

- *Making objects move or disappear and reappear elsewhere.* It is not uncommon for blessed objects or holy artwork to disappear in severe possession cases. In less serious cases, small objects may disappear and then reappear elsewhere in very strange places. This is an inversion of holy angels' ability to affect the physical world.
- *Causing wounds of various kinds to the body.* In oppression or possession cases, superficial wounds are common. These are usually just on the skin and not deep into the flesh. In more serious possession cases, physical maladies and bodily problems may have been caused (or accelerated) by the fallen angels. This is a mockery of God's ability to heal people.
- *Providing hidden information.* This is a favorite method demons use to draw people into relationship with them. They may claim to be a dead loved one or some friendly spiritual force. They usually provide some false comfort, or useful information, early on. Once the person has requested their help enough times, they turn on the person and start telling them what they can and cannot do. This is demonic oppression. The information demons give is usually just a manipulation of the fact that fallen angels can observe and predict many things, or they might predict something and then go and do it themselves so that the prediction seems to have come true. This is not really an inversion of one angelic faculty but may use different faculties for evil.

- *Providing favors in general.* Providing apparent service to people is a common trick used on people practicing Wicca, witchcraft, satanism, or other forms of spiritualism. Accepting this service is a violation of the First Commandment because it is turning to a spirit other than God for information, power, or comfort. The only created spirits that will draw people into breaking their friendship with God are fallen angels. This is why black magic (divination, Ouija boards, psychics, Wicca, witchcraft, reiki, kundalini Yoga, satanism, and any other occult system) is almost always the cause of demonic possession cases. The mindset of magic is "my will be done," and the mindset of Christianity is "Thy will be done."

Conclusions

We can discern between real miracles and demonic counterfeits in a few ways:

- *Does the event draw us closer to God, or closer to some created spirit or ourselves?* Miracles always draw us toward a deeper relationship with God. Miracles confirm the reality of God, and God's love for us. Counterfeits draw us away from God into a focus on created spirits or our own self-importance and power.
- *Does the event cause clarity and peace, or confusion and distress?* Miracles bring comfort, peace, and clarity. Demonic counterfeits may bring temporary satisfaction, but it is short lived. Soon anxiety and inner distress occur. The other hallmark of counterfeits is that they bring confusion as opposed to clarity.

- *Did the event happen through or around people who direct others to God, or people who direct others to themselves?* Counterfeits occur around the latter because God would not manifest a sign to draw people away from Him.

Demonic counterfeits often happen around a person in private, but sometimes they happen publicly in order to draw others into deception. Many people abuse the idea of miracles and simply con people into thinking they have powers. Sometimes fallen angels create their effects in support of these people, often making a more potent lure and trap by combining their spiritual tricks with human deception. We will explore some of these scenarios next.

11

Cults of Personality and False Faith Healers

The idea of a miracle can be a powerful tool for good or for evil. In every generation, groups spring up around unethical charismatic individuals who try to use our fascination with the miraculous for their own ends. Sometimes they even claim to be Jesus reincarnated, or to have received special information or messages from God. Often they claim to have special powers to heal, and sometimes to be able to perform other miracles.

The leader is almost always male, and usually seeks access to the women in the group for sexual gratification. These people generally prey on the vulnerable and socially isolated who have a special need for love and acceptance. They also target the sick and the wounded, promising healing and freedom from fear. A central feature that seems to be universal is that they seek to plunder their members, asking not just for what they have now, but for their possessions to be willed to the leader after their death. In order to do this, they usually separate people from their families and from society, convincing them that the group is more important than anything else.

These leaders and their followers either stabilize their claims and find a way to integrate into society, or they spiral out into apocalyptic predictions and violence. Often when the leaders are still alive, they cause trouble that attracts the attention of law enforcement. If a leader dies, his group usually fades away, or a less megalomaniac member takes over and manages the group in a less dramatic way—or sometimes things get worse.

In addition to the extraordinary leader, the group usually claims to be a superior elite that has secret, powerful information. This powerful tactic of the "mystery cult" has been used for millennia. This bait has been used to start myriad magical groups, cults, and false religions. The goal is to isolate people from worldly concerns (and their money) and get them to give up everything for the group. Since these worldviews are quite outlandish if looked at objectively, the group reveals these "truths" only after periods of indoctrination and conditioning. What would have seemed insane if revealed at the beginning now seems like profound truth.

Perhaps the most famous recent example of the unstable type of cult leader is Charles Manson. He had been in and out of reform school and jail his entire life; then in the late 1960s, he drew in a group of educated and intelligent young people. He espoused an apocalyptic worldview and convinced his followers to commit murder so that the resulting social chaos would elevate him to be the leader of the world. The group imploded when the young people committed murders.

The infamous Jim Jones, as a child, studied Stalin, Marx, Mao, Gandhi, and Hitler. His friends saw him as strange and obsessed with religion and death. He became a charismatic preacher and faith healer in Indiana before moving his group to San Francisco in 1965. The media started to investigate his organization, and he moved them away from scrutiny to a jungle commune in South America. When claims of abuses circulated, Congressmen Leo Ryan traveled to investigate; upon boarding the plane to return, he was shot and killed by members of the cult. It was clear that the cult was imploding. Shortly thereafter, Jones had all 918 members, including 304 children, drink cyanide to kill themselves.

The Heaven's Gate cult had a similar story. The odd founders started the group in the 1970s after meeting in a mental hospital, claiming to be divine beings from a higher level of existence. There were alien and UFO aspects to their narrative, but these changed over time. The members, many of which were in the cult for decades, gave interviews right before their mass suicide. The leader's teachings had spiraled out into the apocalyptic prediction that the world would end after a particular comet passed the earth. In March of 1997 they all committed suicide, in order to reach that higher plane, while the Hale-Bopp comet was near.

Fringe ideas generally only attract the fringe of society, so these strange groups are usually small. Jim Jones attracted more, though, because his madness was ensconced in mainstream Christianity. Over the past few decades, developments in mass media have made conning large numbers of people easier. Christian "evangelists" claim to have special powers and to perform miraculous healings on TV, but the goals are usually the same as always: attach people to a wrongheaded but charismatic leader and separate them from their money.

The cult leader who adopts the language and concepts of Christianity is merely borrowing the credibility that legitimate Christianity has from Jesus Christ and two thousand years of tradition. It is a fraud that makes legitimate Christianity less credible to the world. So often this kind of con relies on "proof-texting" Scripture — that is, taking verses out of context to give incomplete or false impressions. For instance, there might be a great emphasis on verses such as "a person will reap only what he sows," which seems to support the prosperity Gospel message that is commonly used to take money from the poor. When the verse is seen in context, it is clear that it is actually about sin:

> Make no mistake: God is not mocked, for a person will reap only what he sows, because the one who sows for his flesh will reap corruption from the flesh, but the one who sows for the spirit will reap eternal life from the spirit. (Gal. 6:7–8)

What about the crowds who seem to have very real physical reactions to charismatic leaders, especially so-called faith healers? People swoon, fall, convulse, or even laugh or scream uncontrollably. Some ill or crippled people stand and walk briefly or even dance. This is all taken as a confirmation of the special powers of the leader, often framed as channeling the Holy Spirit. Most of this is very likely the power of suggestion, which, when accompanied by true belief in the leader, is far greater than we usually appreciate. The stage hypnotist can, in a short time, cause swooning, movements, laughing, or hallucinations—and this is *without* any devotion on the part of the people. Imagine the power of the mind when suggestion is combined with such devotion. It is important to remember that faith healers carefully choose which people come up for healings on television. The severely ill or paralyzed are not displayed; only those who can overcome their pain briefly through adrenaline are used.

In addition to social and psychological manipulations, demons are sometimes involved. Some of these leaders have been drawn into demonic deceptions themselves, and those spirits add their influence on the people who come to events. When looking at the interviews with some of these leaders after their ministry crashed, it is clear they had abhorrent experiences before they became public ministers. Not all of them have had these, and not all are working with demons, but some seem to be.

While working in psychology in prisons, I met a number of serial killers and sociopathic manipulators. They generally had the attitude that if you fall for their lies, then you are weak and deserve any harm they cause you. The sociopath who finds a way to destroy people openly (and often legally) is no less evil than the one who does so in a criminal fashion; they are both choosing to destroy others for personal gain. The sociopathic personality has a number of traits that can be found in both the criminal and the highly functional religious manipulator:

- Superficial charm
- Lack of remorse and shame
- Insincerity
- Poor judgment
- Pathological egocentricity and incapacity for love
- Lack of genuine emotional reactions to things
- Impersonal and trivial sexual life

One can picture any number of high-profile people who, in hindsight, exhibited some of these traits.

Conclusions

It is particularly cruel to use the promise of miracles as a means to manipulate and exploit people. The Church's canon law guards against the use of spiritual goods, including the hope for a miracle, a manipulative way. Sacramental graces must be provided to those who qualify for them and want to have them, without payment. There can be no personal gain of any kind on the part of the priest, who should function as an extension of the Church and not as an individual. Indeed, trading the things of God for material goods, including money, is the sin of simony, one of the most infamous in Christian tradition.

Conclusion

Science seems to be encroaching on religion; so much more is now understood and explained than in the past. Many things that seemed supernatural are now mundane. What used to be possession is dismissed as epilepsy; what used to be a nightmare spirit is now sleep paralysis; what used to be union with God is now a temporal lobe transient that can be created with magnetic fields; and what used to be a near-death experience is just the brain losing oxygen. These explanations may be true and helpful in some cases, but does that mean they are true in all? Sometimes it seems that there is little or no space left for God in our world.

Of course we eventually bump into the unsolvable problem that we started with: mortality. But is this all there is for Christians to hold on to—a gnawing feeling that death can't have the final word? Are we reduced to an uncomfortable and seemingly irrational faith in the face of a mocking world, and the anemic comfort that they will need God eventually?

Miracles are the currency of the realm here; they are the proofs of God. Jesus used them to prove that the Kingdom of God had come, and He continues to use them in the modern world. The risk is that we approach them too casually or too cynically. If we leave rationality behind and regard miracles only through the lens of unquestioning faith, we can make serious errors that reduce the credibility of the Gospel or, worse, give aid to the demonic. We can endorse something that is a misunderstanding at best, a malicious scam at worst. The peddlers of false healings and magical powers count on that. Is it disrespectful to question, to check things out? Of course not: our reason is what is most like God in us.

We have seen that some stories of miracles are likely legend, that some might have seemed remarkable in the past but are now explainable. Can we say that with time and technology all miracles will be explained? Numerous miracles in this book seem to force us to admit the reality of the supernatural: bread does not turn into flesh; diseases do not instantly disappear without a trace; people do not levitate; the sun does not dance. Either we are all victims of an incredible variety of cons that require hundreds of coordinated lies and hoaxes—or God is at work in the world.

Miracles, of course, are most important to the people they happen to, whose lives are often changed forever. Miracles are an extraordinary grace for them. But we can receive inspiration in hearing or reading of miracles, in letting God speak to us through His actions in the world. Just as the Bible is filled with stories that speak to us two thousand years later, miracles speak to us about God's work and love in the world today. We can learn so much from them and be strengthened for the journey by the comfort they bring.

Real miracles are proofs of God, but we cannot build a faith based only on them. We need a living relationship with God through His Church. The main vehicles of grace are the Word of God and the sacraments, instituted by Christ. The center and goal of Christian faith is a living relationship with Jesus, the Father, and the Holy Spirit.

God has continued to give miracles to the world since the time of Christ; they have not stopped, and we may confidently believe they will never stop. Many are quiet miracles that nobody hears about; others are prominent and shared the world over. Let us hope that these stories inspire the world—beginning with you—to seek God, and to seek that miracle that is beyond all others: salvation.

I will meditate on all thy work,
  and muse on thy mighty deeds.
Thy way, O God, is holy.
  What god is great like our God?
Thou art the God who workest wonders,
  who hast manifested thy might among the peoples.
Thou didst with thy arm redeem thy people,
  the sons of Jacob and Joseph. *Selah*
  (Ps. 77:12–15, RSVCE)

About the Author

Adam Blai, a layman, is a peritus (Church-decreed expert) in religious demonology and exorcism for the Diocese of Pittsburgh. He has also served as an expert in these areas in training priests, deacons, and laity in many other dioceses. He is an auxiliary member of the International Association of Exorcists, a Vatican-recognized Private Association of the Christian Faithful based in Rome. Over fifteen years of working and training in the exorcism ministry, he has witnessed or experienced a number of miracles, some of which he has been appointed to investigate by the Church. He also works in the tribunal of the Pittsburgh Diocese and is pursuing a canon law degree.

Sophia Institute

Sophia Institute is a nonprofit institution that seeks to nurture the spiritual, moral, and cultural life of souls and to spread the Gospel of Christ in conformity with the authentic teachings of the Roman Catholic Church.

Sophia Institute Press fulfills this mission by offering translations, reprints, and new publications that afford readers a rich source of the enduring wisdom of mankind.

Sophia Institute also operates the popular online resource CatholicExchange.com. *Catholic Exchange* provides world news from a Catholic perspective as well as daily devotionals and articles that will help readers to grow in holiness and live a life consistent with the teachings of the Church.

In 2013, Sophia Institute launched Sophia Institute for Teachers to renew and rebuild Catholic culture through service to Catholic education. With the goal of nurturing the spiritual, moral, and cultural life of souls, and an abiding respect for the role and work of teachers, we strive to provide materials and programs that are at once enlightening to the mind and ennobling to the heart; faithful and complete, as well as useful and practical.

Sophia Institute gratefully recognizes the Solidarity Association for preserving and encouraging the growth of our apostolate over the course of many years. Without their generous and timely support, this book would not be in your hands.

www.SophiaInstitute.com
www.CatholicExchange.com
www.SophiaInstituteforTeachers.org